"Compelling reading. . . . The authors, in their use of life stories, . . . have blended story with context, theory with example in ways which demonstrate helpfulness and respect. . . . Helps us all to identify with the universals of the human community, and to know ways we can enhance the journey for each other."

—John M. Schneider, Ph.D., professor and clinical psychologist, author of *Stress, Loss, and Grief*

"An ideal resource for pastoral counselors and ministers. . . . Through concrete examples of diverse kinds of life's losses, O'Neill and Ritter gently guide the reader to a spiritual wholeness."

—Jeannine Gramick, SSND, author of *Homosexuality in the Priesthood and the Religious Life*

"Much like the work of Elisabeth Kubler-Ross' stage theory for working through the losses related to terminal illness, the authors use a stage theory framework and some 60 case studies to enable gay men and lesbians to work through the losses accruing to this community from heterosexism and homophobia."

—J. Michael Clark, Ph.D., founding co-chair, Gay Men's Issues in Religion Group, American Academy of Religion, and author of *A Place to Start: Toward an Unapologetic Gay Liberation Theology* and *A Defiant Celebration: Theological Ethics and Gay Sexuality*

"Clarifies the spiritual dimensions of letting go and coming out and [provides] many stories of lesbians and gay men, taken from the authors' professional and personal experiences. I wish this book had been available when I was first coming to terms with my own sexuality and spirituality."

—Chris Glaser, author of *Coming Out to God: Prayers for Lesbians and Gay Men, Their Families and Friends* and *Come Home: Reclaiming Spirituality and Community as Gay Men and Lesbians*

"Since all of our life images shatter at one point or another, I consider this a 'must' for helping professionals. Anyone dealing with loss will find solace and suggestions, encouragement and examples. Lesbian and gay people will take pride in our efforts against the odds."

—Mary E. Hunt, Ph.D., co-director, Women's Alliance for Theology, Ethics and Ritual, author of *Fierce Tenderness: Toward a Feminist Theology of Friendship*

"*Coming Out Within* shows the way through pain to authentic celebration. . . . How I wish this book had been available when I was younger! Through reading it I have learned to respect my own struggles more fully, and to honor my own survival and that of my gay brothers and lesbian sisters everywhere. Whatever has brought us from rigidity toward openness, from external authority toward personal integrity, from disconnectedness toward interrelatedness, and from self-centeredness toward generativity is certainly cause for profound joy."

—Virginia Ramey Mollenkott, author of *Godding: Human Responsibility and the Bible* and *The Divine: Biblical Imagery of God as Female*

"O'Neill and Ritter explore how life images—those compelling hopes that propel us into adulthood—are precast for us all in the workshops of a heterosexual culture. They then trace, through many vignettes, how the alchemy of grieving cleanses and prepares individuals for more authentic visions and commitments."

—James D. Whitehead and Evelyn Eaton Whitehead, authors of *A Sense of Sexuality: Christian Love and Intimacy* and *The Promise of Partnership: Leadership and Ministry in an Adult Church*

"A timely, wise, and compelling book, packed with true-to-life illustrations. *Coming Out Within* is guaranteed to bring hope and insight to anyone who seeks to transform loss into gain."

—Kittredge Cherry, author of *Hide and Speak: How to Free Ourselves from Our Secrets*

"Pulls no punches. . . . O'Neill and Ritter fit the life experience of lesbians and gay men into sensible, manageable stages. Their thoughtful analysis coupled with stories of hope are exhilarating—they enable us to find meaning in loss, to transform our experience."

—Melvin I. Pohl, chief of Clinical Services, Pride Institute

"O'Neill and Ritter work through the journey form despair to resurgent hope and vitality with subtlety, nuance, realism, and compassion. *Coming Out Within* is one of the clearest voices of hope that I know of for lesbians and gays who feel bewildered and betrayed by their own sexual nature and cheated by a homophobic and uninformed church and society. I hope it is widely read and used."

—Dick Hasbany, editor, *Homosexuality and Religion*

"Rich in wisdom and practical application. . . . Ultimately affirming and optimistic *Coming Out Within* is uncompromisingly realistic about the tough challenges facing lesbians and gay men in their struggle towards inner peace and social acceptance. I recommend it highly."

—Richard J. Woods, O.P., author of *Another Kind of Love: Homosexuality and Spirituality*

Coming Out Within

Coming Out Within

*Stages of Spiritual Awakening
for Lesbians and Gay Men*

Craig O'Neill and Kathleen Ritter

HarperSanFrancisco
A Division of HarperCollins*Publishers*

FIRST EDITION

Library of Congress Cataloging-in-Publication Data

O'Neill, Craig.
  Coming out within : stages of spiritual awakening for lesbians and gay men / Craig O'Neill and Kathleen Ritter. — 1st ed.
          p. cm.
  Includes bibliographical references (p.   ).
    ISBN 0–06–250706–0 (alk. paper)
    1. Gays—Religious life. 2. Bereavement. 3. Gays—Psychology.
  I. Ritter, Kathleen.   II. Title.
  BV4596.G38054 1992
  259'.08'664—dc20   91–55287
                                                                          CIP

---

92 93 94 95 96 ❖ CWI 10 9 8 7 6 5 4 3

This edition is printed on acid-free paper that meets the American National Standards Institute Z39.48 Standard.

To Our Mothers
Mary van Lienden and Wilda Yost

Table of Contents

Acknowledgments

We are deeply indebted to the many lesbians and gay men whose stories of loss and transformation have made this book possible. To these friends, students, parishioners, and counselees who have shared with us their hearts, we are truly grateful.

We also appreciate the support, enthusiasm, and careful work of our editor at Harper San Francisco, Kevin Bentley. His suggestions and wise counsel have enriched this book. We thank Caroline Pincus, Harriet Crosby, and Judy Beck, also of Harper San Francisco, for their help in editing and marketing. Thanks go to our agent, Shari Wenk, for her assistance in the various phases of this project. Pat Tomaras helped with the typing of the initial chapters and Denise Candia saw us through other chapters and several additional drafts. We credit her with the transformation of our writing from pages of tape and arrows to a work worthy of production.

Finally, we thank the people at Chris Brownlie Hospice and our special friends, John Ritter, Walter Pinel, Fred Martin, Anthony Terndrup, Jo Cholet, and Stan Teixeira, for their support and suggestions along the way.

Coming Out Within

Introduction

Coming Out Within focuses on the experience of loss for lesbians and gay men by means of an eight-stage model of loss and transformation. In our experience as a Catholic priest who has worked in an AIDS hospice and with recovering chemically dependent gay men and lesbians, and as a psychotherapist who has served numerous lesbian and gay clients over the years, we have listened to many stories of loss. The individuals we work with have shared with us feelings of not belonging to family, church, or the workplace; grief at losing friends and loved ones to AIDS; and demoralization caused by the fact that they are despised by a significant segment of society. From these stories we have shaped the illustrations found in this book. By sharing in the anguish of these people and watching them confront grief, we have journeyed with them from the initial shock of loss to their spiritual healing and transformation.

We expand upon John Schneider's eight-phase model for transforming loss[1] and adapt that model to lesbian and gay populations. Thus, we give readers what Schneider gave us: a clear understanding of the dynamics of loss, the knowledge and motivation to move toward recovery, and the hope that even the most poignant loss can be a stepping-stone to spiritual transformation.

The concept of the *life image* is crucial to understanding gay losses. Growing up in America for most people is

1

a process of acculturation wherein individuals and their dreams, visions of the future, and life scripts are shaped by values, roles, and cultural myths. These societal shaping forces traditionally are heterosexual in nature and contain images of mommies, daddies, babies, husbands, wives, and opposite-sex couples. Our society ignores taboo images of same-gender couples, gay marriages, lesbian families, or openly gay public officials or religious leaders. The typical images of life in this society guide and mold the internal and external experiences of gay men and lesbians and often set up a condition of incongruence between who they are deep inside and how the culture expects them to live.

Some lesbians and gay men never allow an awareness of this discrepancy to surface to the point that redesigning a life image becomes a necessity. Sometimes, however, gays and lesbians experience intense losses that serve to shatter the hopes, dreams, and assumptions considered intrinsic to their life images. It is for these people, their friends, and their loved ones that *Coming Out Within* is written. This book is meant not as a substitute for professional psychotherapy when the effects of loss become debilitating, but as a companion during this critical time.

Our aim is to bring readers hope and inspiration by providing a vision of personal and spiritual wholeness for lesbian and gay people. By presenting a wide variety of stories to which not only they but their families, friends, and significant others can relate, we hope that all readers will be better able to understand the experience of loss for people of same-gender orientation. In addition to increasing understanding of the dynamics of gay and lesbian loss, *Coming Out Within,* through the use of its eight-phase model and accompanying lessons, graphically illustrates how the process of loss to transformation can be facilitated.

Following the presentations of the model is a discussion in chapter 11 of gay and lesbian spirituality flowing from experiences of loss and the shattering of outworn life images. Lesbians and gay men are invited to journey with their inner and best sense of God. Likewise, they are encouraged to see how their lives are guided by a Wisdom that has formed them from conception and that loves them unconditionally. In step with this personal God, they can come to embrace authenticity, openness, and a growing compassion for other marginalized people. Traditional stories of faith are given new relevance, and the passage from death to resurrection is reinterpreted through the eyes of the gay and lesbian experience of loss and transformation.

The Appendix is devoted to helping lesbian and gay individuals navigate through the loss model by addressing three areas that might hinder their progress and by providing encouragement and advice to make their passage smoother. Suggestions are also given to family and friends to assist them in supporting their loved ones in grieving.

The difference in socialization and societal treatment of the genders has made writing a book for both gay men and lesbians a difficult task. Society sets up different worlds for the genders to reside in and allows women less access to organizational power and to the channels of decision making. While both men and women are subject to vocational role casting, women generally earn less than men for the same work. Further, they are more likely to be sexually harassed on the job and left with the children in the wake of a heterosexual divorce.

While some of the characters found in this book are confronted with issues of gender stereotyping and sex discrimination, we chose to focus the reader's attention on losses that are specifically related to the experience of being gay and lesbian. Rather than complicating the illustrations with double- and even triple-layered losses, such as those incurred by being lesbian, female, and Black, we have concentrated on the particularly lesbian or gay aspects of a loss. We realize that each of the above experiences (being lesbian, female, or Black) has its own flavor of marginalization and oppression, but had we broadened the focus of the illustrations, we might have run the risk of minimizing the uniquely gay or lesbian elements of the loss.

The Life Image

Throughout most of the history of Western civilization, gay men and lesbians have often been thought of as embodiments of evil, creatures of darkness, or carriers of the worst traits of humanity. They have been exiled, excluded, burned at the stake, mutilated, reviled, and murdered in attempts to eliminate them from the species.[1] But perhaps the most effective way of banishing their presence has been to shape the life images of most societies in exclusively heterosexual terms. Life images are models people have of how they expect their lives to proceed. In the process of shaping these images in heterosexual terms, our society has nearly eradicated the gay shamans or wise people of ancient cultures and the acceptable same-gender pairings of Greco-Roman societies. In the place of these, the only choice available is now a world of husbands and wives, fathers and mothers, opposite-gender couples, procreation, and society's "leftovers" of old maids and bachelors, widows and widowers.

It is this sphere that shapes the lives and dreams of heterosexuals as well as gay men and lesbians. It is here that conceptions of what constitutes "normalcy," respectability, and a sense of belonging are delineated in terms of exclusively heterosexual images. For lesbians and gay men, attempting to assimilate into these life images is a setup for disillusionment and ultimately for loss. Trying to become what they are not has a price.

Little girls grow up playing wedding and house, donning white tablecloths to emulate their image of a bride. Little boys play varieties of "manly" roles such as cowboy, construction worker, soldier, or even priest; and boys with sisters are often roped into playing the role of husband and daddy. This heterosexual role imprinting takes place at an early age and sets deep in the psyche the path one will take in life and the measure of normality. From these seemingly simple childhood and adolescent exercises, personal life images are formed and the dream of a future life becomes crystallized.

At age thirty, Alex was still looking for a wife. Over the years his quest for a lifemate had been unrelenting. He had dated several women and enjoyed their companionship, but simply failed to generate any sexual arousal toward them. Desperation began to take hold of him as his failures continued and he became more aware that he might never develop any heterosexual interest. To him, a wife was an integral part of his lifelong vision of marriage, a family, respectability, and normalcy. The thought of never being "normal" in this sense terrified him, and he could see no way out. He finally sought therapy and eventually admitted to having had attractions toward men for most of his life.

The prices that Alex paid for following a dream that was foreign to his nature were many years of living an anguished life and a deep sense of loss. When the heterosexually oriented life image shatters for gay men and lesbians, the losses, like those of Alex, are many and cut to the core of the being. Alongside the loss of "normalcy" are the equally debilitating losses in the areas of family relationships, work, health, religion, and community. Losses in any of these realms can serve to highlight for gay and lesbian people the incongruity between the facts of life and the facts of *their* lives. Caught in the midst of such dissonance, they are in a position to confront their illusion that the predominant societal life image can work for them.

Family

Losses emanating from family relationships are some of the most difficult for gay men and lesbians to face. These losses seem to occur on two fronts: the family of origin and the family one dreams of having.

Family of Origin. Gay men and lesbians are usually accepted within their families of origin as long as they maintain a heterosexual image. Many find that this situation changes drastically as they come out from behind their masks and disclose their orientation. Suddenly, they may become invisible in the eyes of their parents, parents' friends, and siblings. For example, parents of heterosexual adult children generally enjoy telling about their sons- and daughters-in-law and grandchildren, but when the topic of a gay son or lesbian daughter is raised, a parent may fall silent or become evasive, uttering such words as "he's doing all right in his work."

Often the realization dawns on lesbians and gays that they do not belong in their families to the same degree as their siblings. In many cases, these individuals become the black sheep, a family secret, or the one barely whispered about, and this causes their worst fears about who they are to be played out in their own families. In other cases, they simply feel they are second-class members, with married brothers and sisters and their offspring receiving the bulk of parental attention. The family is usually a sure refuge of comfort and esteem for members of other minority groups. But gay men and lesbians, by being relegated to invisibility, to secrecy, or to a second-class citizenship, often experience their deepest losses. They are shorn of that aspect of their life image that leads them to expect a home to be embraced in and a family who affirms and validates their total being.

An extreme illustration of parental invalidation and rejection is that of Paula, who was the last in the line of an Irish Catholic family. She was an only child and neither of her parents had brothers or sisters who reproduced—most had joined religious communities. Her parents were counting on her for continuation of the family history and genetic line and had taken great pains to invest her with family stories to be passed on to her children and children's children. When, after much struggle and many tears, she announced on her twentieth birthday that she was lesbian, her parents kicked her out, told her never to darken their lives with her presence, and prayed for her as for one of the dead.

Familial rejection and accompanying loss is often much more subtle and disguised than the outright discarding that Paula experienced. Because of its subtlety, however, it is often much more damaging to the psyche. Couching expressions of rejection in loving terms confuses people and sets up a system of "crazy-making." For example, a mother telling her son, "I want you to be happy, but I don't want you to be happy as a homosexual," is communicating to the son her rejection of an integral element of his makeup. "I love you but I don't love your being queer" is another illustration of the same kind of a double message. In both instances, parents assume that their children's sexual orientation is like any other behavior of which they disapprove, such as smoking, drinking, clothing, hairstyle, or choice of friends. Gay and lesbian individuals frequently intuit differently, knowing at some level that their orientation is an essential and unchangeable ingredient of their being. They also may realize that there is no way for them to please such parents. By placing a condition upon their love (namely "stop being gay or lose my love") parents set up their children to live a life of pretense. Such parents seem to give their children two choices: either "please yourself and lose me" or "lose yourself and please me."

Children have a natural need to look into their parents' faces and see joy and approval reflected there. They want to be a source of happiness and satisfaction for their mothers and fathers. At some point in their lives, perhaps early on, many lesbian and gay people realize that if they reveal who they are, they not only will miss that look of affirmation but also may experience themselves as a source of parental disappointment and pain. Either way, their life image of family harmony is clouded and there is a deep sense of loss.

An example of a damaged life vision is Robert, who was raised on a farm in Virginia and whose only sibling was a developmentally delayed brother. His father had been grooming Robert to inherit the estate that had been in the family for many generations.

9

Robert's father often would comment that his greatest hope and pride was in his son passing on their productive acres to his children. When Robert, after much internal struggling, told him that he was gay, his father was heartbroken. Robert listened while his father said, "Son, I love you dearly, but as of today I have no further reason to live. You were our only hope. Your mother and I had counted on having grandchildren and passing on our heritage to them through you." Robert still grieves when he remembers the look on his father's face and acknowledges the sadness he unavoidably brought into his family's life.

Sandra's mother's reaction to the news of her daughter's sexual orientation was, "I will go along with your decision to be a lesbian, but it hurts me so much to think of you always being unhappy and being discriminated against." Sandra took issue with her mother, but internally she was feeling helpless to correct her mother's misinformation, bring her any comfort, be a source of maternal joy, or receive any validation for herself.

When lesbians and gay men enter into committed relationships, another dimension is added to that of familial expectation. Consider all the situations so far discussed in this chapter—then include a partner in the equation, and imagine the increased complexity of each. Just as gay and lesbian people want affirmation and respect for themselves, they also desire the same for their partners. Instead of hearing words like "you chose well," they may hear disparaging words such as "you're not bringing her to our home, are you?"

Chelsea and Carrie had been living together for five years in Los Angeles. Chelsea's parents lived in Newport,

Rhode Island, and took enormous pride in gathering their children and large extended family for Christmas each year. Chelsea had talked to many of her family members about her lesbianism, but out of deference to her parents, who still resisted the idea, most of them had chosen not to discuss her orientation. Chelsea dearly desired to introduce Carrie into the family circle much as the wives and husbands of her siblings had been introduced. She told her folks a month before Christmas that if they wanted her presence, they would have to include Carrie as well. Reluctantly, they agreed, since to them it was important to have everyone together.

When they arrived, Chelsea and Carrie noted that Grandmother had been moved to Aunt Connie's home and her bedroom prepared for Carrie. Chelsea was accorded her childhood room on the next floor. This was the first of many examples of refusals to acknowledge their couplehood during the visit. Carrie's name was not included in the family gift exchange. Two of her sisters pulled Chelsea aside and upbraided her for daring to bring her girlfriend to the "family" Christmas; they then took pains to avoid Carrie. Her little brother said he was embarrassed when the two women held hands momentarily during the Christmas Eve church service (even though Chelsea noted that her older brother and his wife were doing likewise). Her Uncle Fred refused to visit at all when he heard that a "dyke" was staying at his sister's house and he said he wasn't going to "condone such perversion" by his presence.

By meeting Carrie, Chelsea's parents were confronted for the first time with the reality of their daughter's lesbianism. Before this, whenever Chelsea visited she was

11

alone, so it was possible for her parents to relegate her orientation to the back of their minds. Seeing Carrie triggered in them a sense of loss of their daughter's normality. Their pain would not allow them to get close to Carrie, which hurt Chelsea deeply. This, coupled with a shattered life image and loss at seeing her parents' anguish, intensified Chelsea's own sense of loss.

It is natural to desire a bond with another human being and then to wish that the partner be loved and accepted by one's own family. When families fail to validate gay and lesbian members and their committed relationships, intense feelings of loss ensue. Just as gay individuals rarely choose their sexual orientation, rarely do they elect to lose the love of their parents; in fact, most go to great lengths to retain it. But at some point, healthy gay men and lesbians must come to accept their orientation and may grieve the dismantling of the life image as it relates to their family, even if that means experiencing the pain of alienation from a family that cannot accept them.

Family of Dreams. The image of the "normal" family is deeply embedded in the human psyche. Regardless of sexual orientation, most people try to match their lives with an almost unconscious blueprint or model of acceptability. Many uncoupled individuals live their lives as though they were "on hold," waiting for that right person with whom to embark on a normalizing process. Any arrangement prior to this relationship is considered temporary, and people often feel deeply flawed if they fail to find their life's partner. Many heterosexual individuals find themselves in this situation, but, unlike lesbians and gay men, they often do not realize until much later in life that their dream of connectedness will never materialize. People of same-gender orientation tend to arrive at this awareness much earlier, since any intimate relationship they envision is considered by most of society to be shameful, unacceptable, certainly nonsacramental, ultimately fragile, and something to be hidden from polite society. In other words, gay and lesbian people mourn that an intimate relationship, which they consider an entry point into a "normal" life, will not be as they had dreamed. This loss can initiate them into a downward spiral of other losses as they realize that the family of their life image will not materialize.

Diane is the youngest of five daughters, her mother's "unexpected treasure," as she was born considerably later than the other four. She watched as her older sisters married and left home. She served as either flower girl or bridesmaid for each, and she would often be asked to babysit the growing number of nieces and nephews. All this reinforced how she would be living her dreams someday. An attraction toward men never evolved. In fact, in her fantasies she was always loved by beautiful women in the persons of TV and film stars and her teachers. The women whom she most admired and wished to emulate in her community had relationships with men and not with women, and this distressed her deeply. Thus the usual entry point to the life that she had imagined, namely, a heterosexual marriage, was closed to her, and with it the dreams of marriage and children she had so fondly nurtured as a young girl began to dissolve.

Until recently, with the advent of artificial insemination and nontraditional parenting options, the avenues to parenthood for gay men and lesbians were restricted to children from a former marriage or an occasional foster child. The desire to nurture and care for one's own is strong in most human beings, and gay men and lesbians are no exception. Most lesbians and gays feel a deep loss when they realize that they will never be parents. This loss can recur and present itself in different forms as a person ages—from the initial shattering of a childhood dream of being a mother or father to the aching loneliness of old age with no offspring to ease its passage.

While Diane's example illustrates the early dissolution of a girlhood life image, the case of Richard exemplifies the mid-life recurrence of this loss. Richard thought he had come to grips with a lifetime of childlessness. During his early twenties he had sought counseling to deal with this loss, and he felt that he had reached resolution at a level sufficient to turn his energies to the establishment of a career. Shortly after his thirtieth birthday, he met Mark, with whom he went about putting together a life like the one he had envisioned in childhood, except that his partner was a man instead of a woman. Their love and life together prospered, and soon they had a mortgage, furniture, pets, and other symbols of an American suburban lifestyle. In the midst of all this, Richard began experiencing periods of deep depression, and, at age thirty-nine, he again sought professional help. He came to see that he was feeling a profound need to nurture a child, much as he and Mark were nurturing each other. He asked himself why he and Mark were working so hard—to whom would they pass on the fruits of their labor? He experienced a need to reach beyond himself and contribute to and mentor the next generation.

Regardless of how well or poorly people resolve the

generativity issue at mid-life, it is bound to surface again as aging occurs. People without blood or genetic connections often feel like adopted children, without a sense of who they are or where they came from. This situation is particularly true of many older gay men and lesbians who find themselves starkly alone with generational connectedness disrupted on all sides.

Anita, age sixty-three, once imaged herself surrounded by a home and children of her own. While growing up in Kentucky during World War II and its aftermath, she realized that she was different from her peers but lacked the vocabulary or experience to describe her feelings. Had she lived on either coast, she might have found the support of a burgeoning lesbian community; in the heartland of America, she found none. So she spent her adult years in confusion, denial, and inner loneliness, while consuming copious cups of coffee and being everyone's favorite Aunt Anita. She never claimed herself as a lesbian—such a title was foreign to her—but she liked the chummy company of other women, enjoyed her work at the hardware store, was a star on the bowling team, and never had much interest in marriage. In spite of a seemingly full life, she intuited that there was a void within her; this became more apparent as she buried her parents, her older brothers and sisters, and a few of her acquaintances. The death of her best friend was the last straw. Without parents, siblings, or her closest connection, the aloneness and loss were almost too much to bear. She became aware that she missed children of her own and the deep satisfaction of passing on a part of herself and her experience to her own flesh and blood. She was able to move on with the support of her friends at the store and on the bowling team, but she continued to grieve for the family she would never have.

Most humans foster an image of themselves in a family of their own rather than playing the role of the constant visitor, the perpetual outsider, or everyone's favorite aunt or uncle. They want to picture themselves as a link in a chain, passing a heritage from one generation to another and seeing themselves replicated in another human being. Many gay men and lesbians, at various points of their lives, grieve over this lack of generational relatedness. Even though their friendship bonding may be deeply satisfying, mourning for the lost image of a family replays itself like a sad, wordless melody throughout life.

Work

Sexual orientation can be a key factor in how lesbians and gay men envision themselves in a work environment, feel about their occupations, and perform in their jobs. This life image manifests itself differently among various groups. The following are five categories of gays and lesbians:

1. those who feel so broken early on in life that they are no longer able to hope or to imagine that anything they plan will materialize

2. those who can still dream but fail to realize their potential due to prejudicial treatment in their work environment **or** to a realistic appraisal of their work situation and the futility of achieving upward mobility as a lesbian or gay individual

3. those who may have wanted to "be something"

when they grew up but whose fear of exposure keeps them hidden and thus underemployed relative to their talents and skills

4. those whose vocational plans are interrupted by their inability to focus energy away from issues related to their sexual orientation

5. those who truly achieve the substance and trappings of their life images but at the price of pretense and incongruity

We concur with some of the more recent thinking that societal trauma directed toward gay men and lesbians is experienced by the survivors in much the same way as if the trauma had been inflicted by a specific person or circumstance. The way that gay people describe their feelings resulting from their being abused by society is often similar to the way neglected, abused, and abandoned children describe theirs. As is the case with abused children, the self-image of lesbians and gay men and their ability to project a life image have usually been damaged to some extent. This disruption has varying effects on their vocational paths. The following sections will illustrate these variations of work patterns.

The Brokenhearted. In some cases, early loss interacts with the effects of sexual orientation to produce individuals who suffer from lifelong disillusionment. Children from alcoholic homes, those who have been battered or abused, and sometimes even adopted children feel such an early sense of parental abandonment that they rarely feel good about anything. These dynamics, when combined with the oppression that society inflicts on those with a same-gender sexual orientation, often result in the

17

failure to develop a life image that contains any vocational identity. These individuals, who have so often had their dreams shattered, have the emotional sense that they cannot trust the future not to break their hearts one more time. They protect themselves by saying, "Don't get your hopes up."

Tony started saying this very early in life. His father had worked for years in a steel mill in Allentown, Pennsylvania, and was a hard-drinking, quick-tempered, harsh disciplinarian who often took out his own anger at life on Tony. His mother had a serious heart problem and was often in bed during Tony's formative years. He had a vague sense of her love for him but absorbed more of her despair and sadness; this made him a quiet, sensitive child. Because of this and his small stature, his father would torment him and try to "make a man out of him." When Tony failed to perform adequately, his father would call him a "fag."

When Tony was fourteen, his mother died and his father's drinking as well as his physical and verbal abuse intensified. At least while Mom was alive, there was some protective presence that attracted Tony to stay. After her death, he ran away to New York City. He had earlier begun to realize that his father's worst accusations were true and that he was indeed a "fag." From others in the city like himself he learned that, in order to stay alive, he had to sell either his body or drugs. While he was working the streets, some members of an organization for runaway children befriended him. They offered him food and a place to stay, as well as vocational and educational training. But Tony's fear of getting his hopes up and his heart broken again made him mistrust their goodwill.

Rejecting their practical help, he said "once a fag, always a fag" and returned to the streets.

The Underachievers. Most lesbian and gay people are quite capable of formulating a vocational life image and taking the steps necessary to realize it. All individuals who are pursuing a career that has been a lifelong dream experience disillusionment and the need to reformulate ambitions and expectations at many points in their lives. The difference between gay or lesbian and heterosexual people, however, is that the former often experience disillusionments and occupational shifts due strictly to their sexual orientation. These are over and above the normal ebb and flow of personal and vocational life, such as parental and sibling deaths; declining health, burnout, and so on.

The workplace can be excessively cruel to gay and lesbian individuals. Homophobia is an ever-present and potent reality in many organizations. Untold numbers of gays and lesbians have been given dishonorable discharges from the military. Catholic priests and nuns, Protestant ministers, Jewish rabbis, and seminarians of all denominations have been quietly dismissed, transferred, and sometimes ostracized by their churches. Gay and lesbian police personnel, teachers, and other public and private sector employees have been harassed, embarrassed, and often passed over for promotion. One rarely, if ever, hears of an openly lesbian or gay mayor (except in West Hollywood), university president, corporation CEO, Supreme Court justice, school district administrator, or presidential candidate. In fact, in those work situations where the male patriarchal system establishes the norms, men who aspire to the top positions usually must have a woman beside them lest they give the appearance of being gay. (Similar rules do not hold for women, because women seldom make it to the top of the patriarchal pyramid.) Thus, many gay men and lesbians underachieve, not for lack of talent or hard work, but because many organizations simply will not allow them to achieve their life images.

In this same vein, some gay and lesbian people are realists and see that the chances of achieving their dreams of success and position are truly limited given the homophobic attitudes found in much of the workplace. For those individuals, underachievement often can be explained by a realistic appraisal of their nonexistent chances for recognition and reward.

Carl is an example of a person who was determined to keep his life image intact and not live as a professional underachiever. He had an early love of numbers and how things work, and he delighted in explaining these matters to his chums in the neighborhood. He trained to be a math teacher and was employed as such when he met his first computer and immediately switched to the newly emerging field of computer science. When a new high school, complete with a state-of-the-art computer lab, was opening and looking for a teacher who could motivate bright and enthusiastic students, Carl knew he was the one for the job. He loved teaching and computers and was voted yearly by the students as one of the school's most inspirational teachers. About the time the new school was recruiting faculty, whispers about his sexual orientation and relationship with another man reached the ears of school board members. His application for the new position was mysteriously denied. A friend who was privy to the "inside" information of the board reported to Carl that he would never be given a job of any visibility within the school district and, in fact, that he might be "demoted" out of computer science and into freshman math.

Carl had to make a decision about the quality of professional life that he was willing to live. He could stay with the school district and remain closeted, fearful, resentful, and underutilized, or he could seek a job where his orientation was not a shameful secret. His integrity led him to apply and be accepted into a large computer organization where his sexuality was not an issue in hiring. He found himself tolerated in his new career but soon discovered that this personal acceptance did not guarantee professional advancement. As his peers ascended the corporate ladder, he remained where he had started as a programmer in the computer pool.

This corporate dead end compelled him again to make a career choice based on his sexual orientation. He realized that in only a limited number of professions, such as the arts or social services, could an openly gay or lesbian person work comfortably, be promoted, and achieve full potential within an organization. Given his love for computers, need for personal integrity, and strong desire to realize his life work, he told himself that the only option was to work for himself in a large city. He moved to Houston and started a business as a computer consultant.

The Underemployed. Fear constitutes one of the major reasons for lesbian or gay underemployment. Having heard the horror stories of openly gay people being hounded, harassed, demoted, or fired by management, many gay men and lesbians choose not to undergo this treatment and keep their identity a secret. They spend their entire vocational lives in the closet, fearful of nearly any form of publicity, spotlight, or promotion that may cause them to be exposed. They may choose jobs as bus drivers, mechanics, assembly line workers, cashiers, clerks, typists in a corporate pool, or cleaning service employees. While these are worthwhile vocations for those whose temperament and talents are suited to them, they are selected by many gay and lesbian individuals because they offer escape from interactions that might lead to detection. Work in which encounters with others are limited in range, prescribed by role, and restricted to exchanging information about the business at hand can serve to keep lesbian and gay people hidden. Often, those electing these professions are basically extroverted personalities, but fear compels them into a work choice that is often incompatible with their more person-oriented nature.

Likewise out of fear, gay and lesbian individuals may select jobs that do not reflect their intellectual capabilities. At some point in their lives, they may have aspired to "be something." They may have had a life image of themselves in a particular occupation, but they became afraid and thus limited their willingness to risk, challenge themselves, or compete, ending up in work that underutilizes their talents.

Georgia remembers her high school days, when she was infatuated with her softball coach, Miss Adams, and wanted to be just like her. This image of a career in sports started when she was in grade school and devoted much of her time to softball leagues and tournaments. Her dream crystallized as she watched Miss Adams inspire the members of her teams to reach beyond themselves. It was at this time that Georgia realized that she was lesbian. The terror and shame of this awareness shattered the vision and caused her to believe that someone as damaged as she was couldn't afford to get her hopes up. This was underscored by the occasional taunts she would receive from the others girls in the locker room about her being in love with Miss Adams. The teasing and rumors humiliated her and led her to vow that, at no time in the future, would she ever place herself in such a vulnerable position. As a result, she never again even entered a locker room.

Georgia won a full academic scholarship to college, and when the time came to try out for the softball team, she refused. Without the spark of ambition that athletics had provided, and without its support network, she drifted away from college in her first year and took a job as a gas station attendant, sitting in a locked booth on the night shift. Ten years later she still works that job.

Not all gay men and lesbians who work in more solitary occupations like Georgia's are there out of fear of society's harassment. Some lesbian and gay people, just like heterosexuals, are introverted and naturally gravitate toward work that requires very little socialization. In addition to those occupations listed above, this group might include artists and crafts people, cowboys and cowgirls, forestry workers, wilderness guides, sheepherders, writers, musicians, and carpenters.

If these more isolated occupations are chosen freely out of genuine love of the work and are not simply responses to fear and shame, and if they are congruent with the individual's personality type, then they constitute healthy vocational choices. Too many gay and lesbian people, however, are restrained by fear alone from ever achieving their vocational life images or intellectual potential.

The Shifters. For many gay men and lesbians, dealing with their sexual orientation consumes much of the energy that ordinarily would be devoted to vocational imaging and preparation. Developmentally, heterosexual people begin addressing their sexuality with the advent of puberty, so by the time they emerge into the workplace after high school or college, they are no longer expending inordinate amounts of energy integrating their sexuality into their lives. Due to denial and repression, lesbian and gay people may not begin to deal authentically with who they are as sexual beings until the time when the culture asks them to make plans for vocational life. Some (who will be discussed in the next section) postpone coming to grips with their sexuality and concentrate on their life dreams and ambitions. Others attempt to devote energy and attention both to the issues of their sexual orientation and to the pursuit of their life work, which often results in a fitful series of vocational starts and stops. Within this cycle of highs and lows, gay men and lesbians can begin to experience a loss of themselves as "alive" beings and despair that they may never again feel vitality. They fear that they are "losing it" and may never find work that is perpetually challenging and satisfying. Shifting usually continues until these individuals accept the fact that they are lesbian or gay and test that awareness with others on a personal, public, and physical level. As we will see in the case of Alice, it is not uncommon for gay men and lesbians to envision and take on new projects, get their hopes up, and then lose this enthusiasm over and over again.

Alice never seemed to be able to find her niche in life. Other kids seemed to know what they wanted to be when they grew up, but she cannot remember ever imagining herself as an adult. Growing up, she would start many projects only to quickly abandon them. A constant element to all these girlhood endeavors, however, was that they involved working creatively with her hands. She seemed to excel at handicrafts and art but could never sustain enough interest to finish any of the projects. She floated through high school suspecting that she was different from other kids. It was not until near her graduation that Alice was able to give a name to this difference. She was so confused and troubled that complexities such as selecting a college and major were too much for her, so she stayed home and took basic courses at the community college.

As with the projects of her childhood, Alice would begin classes only to drop them or finish with low grades. This led her eventually to drop out of college and take a series of low-paying jobs. She soon lost interest in all of these, so she again entered college with renewed enthusiasm, only to lose momentum as she had so many times before. But then, in a women's study course, she met other lesbians and started hanging around with them. As a result of these new friendships and the acceptance she felt from these women, she developed an appreciation of herself as lesbian and of the life-giving quality of bonding between women. With this newfound support and validation, Alice found herself better able to sustain her interest in her courses. Her friends were impressed by her talent and encouraged her to pursue an art major, which she eventually completed. After graduation, she found rewarding work with a commercial art firm. Being pleased with the reception that private galleries were according her work, she began to entertain hopes of eventually devoting herself full time to her painting.

The Pretenders. Some lesbians and gay men achieve success in the workplace at the expense of their integrity. They pretend that they are not who they are and, as a result, live distant from their inner beings, often in a world of fear and denial. The trappings of success that come with buying into a heterosexually based life image are exchanged for the turmoil of incongruity and the pain of living separated from their souls. Peter Tchaikovsky described this well when he said, "All that is left is to pretend. But to pretend to the end of one's life is the highest torment."[2]

Gregory was an only child who was doted upon by his parents, both of whom impressed upon him the need to succeed and make a name for himself. He first became aware of his sexual orientation in high school, but both the terrible shame of this and his desire to become student body president made him suppress his inclinations and pretend to be hotly interested in a number of the more popular girls. He maintained the image into college in order to be accepted into the most upscale fraternity. While living in the fraternity house, he began a relationship with one of the other men, and by graduation they were deeply in love. He and Ted talked about spending their lives together. But when the time came for Gregory to meet with a recruiter from a major corporation for which he had always desired to work, he knew he had to make a choice between his love and his life image of success. Without the appearance of heterosexuality, Gregory knew that he had no hope of ascending the corporate ladder. The pain he felt when he broke up with Ted was intense, but he knew he could not let it deter him from following his ambitions for power and financial success. He shut Ted out of his life and pretended that their college days together were a perverse "phase" of his development.

With the proper job within his grasp, he decided to shop around for the right wife to help him advance in his career and found her in the daughter of the CEO of his corporation. They married, had two daughters, and began to assimilate the lifestyle of affluence and good breeding. In spite of a seemingly successful life, with corporate promotions and glittering parties, Gregory experienced an inner torment and occasional flashbacks to his days of happiness with Ted. At some level, he knew he was a gay man at heart and that he had sold his integrity for the corporate dream of success.

Rather than being an arena for self-enhancement, for many gay men and lesbians work becomes an arena for loss. Rather than completing themselves through their life work or a life project, lesbian and gay individuals are often compromised vocationally. The trauma of living with an identity that is so denigrated by the majority of society can leave some people of same-gender orientation so compromised that they cannot see themselves in any life work, so fearful that they hide their talents in obscurity, so discriminated against that they fail to realize even a part of their life image, so disoriented that they cannot sustain a sense of vision or inner joy about what they do, or so

27

disassociated that they fail to come to terms with their true identities.

Health and Safety

When charting a life map, most people take the maintenance of good health and personal safety for granted. Everyone experiences some loss of health as an integral part of the aging process; indeed, anyone can experience health impairment or an accident at any given age. But a life image that presumes good health is particularly precarious, problematic, and insecure for gay and lesbian individuals due to the rising threats of violent attacks and AIDS.

Violent Attacks. Assaults on gay men and lesbians are increasing and coming more frequently to the attention of law enforcement officials. Violence directed toward gay people is a sad reality in America, although it seems that crimes against gay men and lesbians are reported far less often than crimes such as robbery and murder. This may be due to the victims' unwillingness to be public about their orientation or to their fear of harassment, prejudice, or misinterpretation from the police and criminal justice system.

Sarah and Joanne had been dancing at a local bar that catered to both gay men and lesbians. Upon driving away from the bar, they noticed that they were being followed by a carload of what appeared to be men. Sarah noticed that the car was still behind her after she dropped Joanne at her apartment, so she rolled up the windows and locked her doors. She remained on well-lit main avenues until she thought she had ditched the pursuers. Feeling that she was safely away from them, she drove to her small house, set well back from a darkened street in a grove of trees. As she was about to insert her key into the front door, she was surprised by footsteps behind her and a large hand covering her mouth. She was forced inside and pushed to the floor by four men whose faces were covered by ski masks. Two tied her down while the other two trashed her house, spraypainted her walls with words like "queer," "dyke," and "lesbo," and destroyed her property. While this was occurring, the other two verbally abused her and methodically cut off the buttons of her blouse, ripped her skirt, and slapped her around. The noise of the attackers and the crashing of furniture caused the neighbor's dogs to bark, which prompted the man next door to come investigating with his flashlight. Before the punks had a chance to follow through on their promises "to give her a taste of real sex," they noticed the neighbor in the yard. One of the attackers kicked her viciously in the stomach and then joined his buddies as they crawled out a side window.

The neighbor was able to enter through the unlocked front door and released Sarah. Her first words were, "Don't call the police." She told him that she didn't want the details of her assault to reach the local newspaper, which had a reputation for putting the sexual orientation of people into its headlines. Further, she knew that such disclosure might lead to problems, possibly firing, at her job.

The neighbor, however, had already notified the police when he first heard the noises next door. The police arrived and subjected her to an investigation that made her feel that she was the guilty party. She was asked what she had done to attract these men to her house. When she told them about first seeing the men following her from the bar, the policeman asked if that was the bar where women danced with each other. The tone of his voice and his glance at his partner indicated to Sarah that he was amused and not taking her situation very seriously. He seemed to discount her story about not being raped and asked her endless details about the sexual aspects of the attack. When they departed, Sarah was humiliated and had the feeling that little would come of their investigation. And indeed, she was correct.

Incidents such as Sarah and Joanne's are being described more frequently in the gay community and press and to some extent affect the way lesbians and gay men see their future. These stories jeopardize their ability to incorporate the elements of relative safety and good health necessary for the formulation of a positive life image.

AIDS. Acquired Immune Deficiency Syndrome (AIDS) has claimed the lives of thousands of people, particularly gay men. The losses associated with this disease penetrate directly to the core of the human psyche. In a sense, the very viability of the life image is shattered and all that a person had hoped and dreamed for is suddenly erased as a possibility for the future. The disease often strikes those who are at the beginning of their adult journeys and imposes upon them developmental tasks that are beyond their years. Often, youthful individuals are being asked to confront issues that previously were reserved for the elderly, who had lived through enough years of accumulated losses and learned that they could transcend and grow through them. These young men are thus required

30

to mature rapidly, and not all of them are up to the task. So many losses in so short a period age the soul, particularly if the person harboring the AIDS virus has watched many of his friends wither and die.

A sinister aspect of the disease is the toll it takes on the confidence that one's body will function and heal itself, will pull through and succeed at the tasks that life is presenting, and will actualize the images one has for the future. This despair is often combined with a feeling of self-contamination or, for those who are virus-negative, the fear of being contaminated. Also connected with this disease is the feeling of shame—the shame of contracting an illness that society seems to brand as morally reprehensible. Some feel the shame of having to come out as gay in addition to the humiliation of having fallen victim to a sexually transmitted disease.

The best way to deal with this illness is usually with the support of friends, but for gay men in an era of AIDS, the safety net of buddies often unravels. With many of their companions either sick, dead, or too psychically weary to respond, many gay men find themselves virtually alone. However, after a time of historical estrangement between gay men and lesbians, the latter, seeing the suffering of the men and realizing that these are their people, have frequently befriended their brothers. By doing so, they have come to share in the anguish of the loss.

Sean's story highlights some of the losses identified with the gay community in the age of AIDS. Hearing that gay males who had been even minimally active sexually should consider a blood test for the antibodies to the AIDS virus, Sean went to the testing center with confidence that he would test negative. When the test came back positive, Sean was devastated. He was convinced that some mistake had occurred in testing and was numb when a second test confirmed the results of the first. He tried to ignore it for a time, but eventually he shared it with three friends, one of whom, Robert, admitted that he likewise had tested positive and was now beginning to show symptoms. Of the other two friends, Phil had tested positive but was unable to come to terms with that fact, and the other friend, from that day onward, withdrew from Sean, not wishing to become emotionally contaminated.

Sean and Robert had heard of experimental treatment programs and support groups for virus-positive men in Chicago, but that was too far away from their rural home. So the two of them were left to see each other through their ordeal together. Thus, the scared and anxious twenty-eight-year-olds began to take turns comparing symptoms or the lack thereof, much as might men forty years older than they. Robert's illness was further advanced, and he needed to take time from work for frequent visits to the clinic for blood tests and treatments for an increasing array of ailments. He eventually exhausted his "sick days" at work and was docked for additional missed time. Sean remained supportive but interiorly was terrified at the thought of it happening to him. While Sean was convalescing from what seemed to be a cold that held on too long, he heard news of Phil's sudden hospitalization. He visited Phil in the hospital and was shocked to discover his friend near death with AIDS and still denying the presence of the virus because he was too ashamed to admit it. Phil's death was a crippling blow to both Sean and Robert, from which neither ever really recovered. Soon after this, Robert was forced to quit his job and became embroiled in a complicated series of entanglements with governmental agencies and insurance companies in order to provide compensation sufficient for his care and well-being. This sapped him of what little energy he had left. In the events of Robert's life, Sean saw the handwriting on the wall. Soon his symptoms increased, his job became compromised, and his condition resembled that of Robert's.

In order to qualify for public assistance benefits, these men had to sell all their possessions, which left them empty, demoralized, and with confidence shattered. They knew they had to tell their parents, give up their illusory independence, and move home. Both put this off as long as possible. Robert's condition worsened to the point that he couldn't care for himself, and he had to let his family know that he had AIDS and needed a place to stay. The day he stood on the curb and waved goodbye to Robert was the worst day of Sean's life. He knew that he had no future, no close friends to look after him, and no place to go but home to his parents, who despised his sexual orientation. Even the day Robert died wasn't as dark as this one.

Human beings are whole organisms whose parts are intimately connected; the effects of one's health ripple throughout this organism, affecting not only the physical but also the psychic and spiritual dimensions. For gay men and lesbians, living with constant threats to the self causes an imbalance, a protective vigilance that often results in a state of chronic tension that drains energy from productive living. The gay community has often been noted for its artistic vitality and zest for living, which paradoxically has flourished in spite of the often fearful conditions under which gay men and lesbians have had to live for centuries. The onset of AIDS has, in a sense, become the straw that broke the camel's back, leaving gay people who are close to the epidemic with nowhere to go for escape. The constant mourning, the repeated losses with little time for recovery, the continual anxiety of the worried healthy ones, and the drain on caretakers and survivors is decimating internal resources. Existing life images have been demolished, and future life plans have been placed on permanent hold.

Religion

In spite of some condemnatory interpretations of Sacred Scripture, early Christianity was relatively tolerant of homosexuality. It was only in the latter half of the twelfth century that greater hostility began to be directed toward individuals of same-gender orientation. This intolerance was concurrent with the rise of discrimination toward any people who deviated from the standards of the majority, including such groups as the Jews, non-Christians, practitioners of witchcraft, and heretics.[3] This intolerance has been perpetuated and codified in the moral, theological, and legal thinking that continues its influence to this day. While many individuals in church groups are striving to rectify this institutionalized, ecclesial homophobia, the official position in most denominations is harshly judgmental toward same-sex behavior and usually gender orientations as well. Studies have shown that the majority of believers within Christian churches assimilate these doctrines wholesale, accept them as valid, and perpetuate this emotional exiling and denigrating of gay men and lesbians.

While some lesbians and gay men grow up with no religious bonding, many of those who do come to feel like abandoned children. When they look to their religions for an affirmation of their inherent goodness, a sense of community and belonging, and a viable pathway to a Creator, they often come away empty-handed. They find that Mother Church and Father God have deserted them, purportedly attending to other wayward children while making it clear that gay sons and lesbian daughters are to be considered virtual nonmembers of their ecclesial families. This abandonment can undo the spiritual life images of gays and lesbians, leaving them feeling homeless, deserted, unloved, rejected, unlovable, shamed, and enraged.

Affirmation of Goodness. Judeo-Christian belief posits that humans are created in God's image and likeness, that deep in their souls the Creator is reflected. Same-gender orientation is thought by many professionals to be a naturally occurring and sequential process initially facilitated by prenatal brain hormone patterns.[4] Yet most organized religions treat the phenomenon as unnatural, morally reprehensible, objectively disordered, and, as such, something for which one must repent. Asking people to repent for a condition of their very nature thrusts them into a powerful double bind: to engage in a constant struggle against core feelings of rightness and integrity or, on the other hand, to live as outcasts, feeling sinful. Crucial to a viable spiritual life image is a belief of being loved by a loving Creator. Feeling no way out of their double bind, many lesbian and gay people are left with a spiritual vision of disconnectedness and alienation from the Divine. As many gay men and lesbians imagine their future, they do not see God walking with them.

Fernando, who was in his mid-twenties, realized at an early age that he was far more physically attracted to men than to women. His fantasies of falling in love with another man were fulfilled when he met Manuel and they became sexually and emotionally involved with each other. Even though he treasured his relationship with Manuel, his guilt and his fear for his eternal salvation tormented him, finally driving him to his pastor for guidance. The pastor listened sympathetically to his dilemma, called him "my son," and told him that God was always ready to welcome home repentant sinners. All Fernando had to do was give up his homosexuality, much like an alcoholic gives up drinking, and then the gracious Lord would again love him and forgive his sins. The pastor reminded him that "we are never given a cross too great for us to bear" and that Fernando's cross would be to "resist the temptations of homosexuality." The pastor next sent him to a workshop entitled "Christ Can Lead You Out of Homosexuality," where he spent three days listening to speakers describing the evils of a homosexual lifestyle, God's punishment of AIDS, and the inevitability of burning forever in hell for unrepented homosexual acts.

Fernando felt deeply that his love with Manuel was holy and good, but the unrelenting assault of the workshop and the follow-up meetings created a conflict within him, making him distrust his own sense of rightness. As time went on, his fear for his salvation intensified, because, while he had broken up with Manuel, he could not forget the warm tenderness he had felt when he and Manuel had made love. No matter how hard he prayed and followed the advice of his church counselors, the feelings remained with him. He knew he truly was a gay

36

man and thus would always be an unrepentant sinner in the eyes of God and the church and certainly unworthy to be called one of God's children. Depressed and ashamed, he vowed to continue to fight the good fight not to give in to any expression of his sexuality or to embrace the life image that at some level he knew was authentically his own. This constant struggle left him nervous, fragmented, and continually drained.

Sense of Community. One of the benefits of membership in an organized religion is the feeling of sharing life images with others.[5] This support and inclusion rarely extends to openly gay and lesbian individuals, but as long as their sexual orientation is not acknowledged, flaunted, discussed, exposed, or in any way made an issue of, they are sometimes tolerated and even included in church groups. To be truly included, however, lesbians and gay men must maintain an illusion of asexuality in the minds of the other members. Let the orientation become known or in any way spotlighted, and they are often ostracized, snubbed, excluded, or badgered with prayers for conversion.

Lydia had been active in youth ministry ever since she entered high school. Ten years later, her life image still included the love and support of her Christian community. Over the years, she had been active in bringing the word of God to the unchurched, runaways, disturbed youth, the addicted, and the homosexual. She felt she was a part of a loving, supportive community that would stand by her no matter what.

During the course of Lydia's involvement with the youth group, she had been somewhat detached from her own sexual feelings, sublimating them by redoubling her

37

efforts for the group. She sensed that these feelings were wrong in the eyes of her church and that the way to deal with them was to deny them and continue to live in a Christ-like manner. This worked until, at age twenty-four, she met Adrianne and was swept off her feet. She was extremely confused and guilt-ridden and knew she needed to talk to someone. She remembered that her group had recently prayed for the conversion of an openly lesbian counselor at the local college, and she turned to this woman for help. The counselor gave her validation, shared with Lydia her own similar struggles, and supplied her with lesbian-affirming literature. Gradually she came to know other lesbians and joined a support group through which she met her counselor's partner. Through these experiences, she came to see that what she had learned about the "homosexual lifestyle" was false.

As a part of her development, Lydia felt she needed to share her life with her old friends in the youth group. Two of them told her that they didn't understand but that they would continue to love her. Another said he would still love her but would pray that she could be released from this evil. The fourth person in whom she confided told the leader, who promptly called a meeting of the officers of the youth group to determine how to deal with this problem in their midst. They made a vow of secrecy so as not to scandalize the rest of the believing community. Since Lydia had been a role model for many young people, it was considered important that the nature of her fall from grace not be known. Unless she repented and converted from homosexuality, the officers saw no way that she could continue to participate in their ministry. Lydia was deeply hurt by what she considered to be the betrayal of the mutual promises made between her and the group to be supportive through life's adversities. With that betrayal, she witnessed the demise of an expectation that she and her religious community would be bonded for life.

Pathway to the Creator. When the church of one's heritage fails to affirm a sense of goodness or to provide a feeling of community, the result frequently is overwhelming loss. Intensifying this feeling of abandonment for many lesbians and gay men is the crumbling of a life image that included the ability of their faith to provide them with a road map to the Divine.

Most organized religions are permeated with institutionalized heterosexuality, which is exemplified in their shaping stories and role models, spiritual interpretations, and clerical selection processes, as well as in the makeup of most parish or congregational organizations. Sacred Scripture highlights few models of same-sex love and friendship, and as we have pointed out elsewhere, "never is a sexually intimate relationship between two people of the same sex used as an example of perfect or divine love."[6] Most stories of saintly lives focus either on heterosexually focused ways of living or on virginity and celibacy as the only pathways to God. So gay and lesbian questers are offered no synthesizing life images that show a reconciliation between a spiritual commitment and same-gender sexual orientation. Gay and lesbian people are singled out in scriptural interpretation only to show them in a pejorative light, casting them outside the realm of God's love and on a pathway to damnation.

The selection process for the ministry also provides no viable pathways for gay men or lesbians, since the only two choices available require a certain level of pretense.

The underlying presumption in both cases is one of heterosexuality: either accepting it in marriage or renouncing the expression of it in celibacy. This lack of inclusion also manifests itself on the level of the local church, where most congregational events, social and otherwise, assume that everyone is heterosexual.

Martin had long experienced a deep spiritual calling, which he interpreted as a call to the ministry. Upon graduation from college, he applied to a divinity school, and in the entrance interview he was asked about his plans "to take to himself a wife." Being gay, he had no such intentions, but, of course, he could not tell this to the school if he wanted to gain entrance. He felt pressures, both subtle and overt, from the very start of his seminary studies, and he soon realized that if he hoped to be called to ordained ministry and to be accepted by a congregation, a wife was essential. It became increasingly evident that he was walking into a dead end, and at the beginning of his second year, he withdrew.

Still at loose ends and still feeling called to God's service, he started investigating those denominations that either mandated or allowed a celibate clergy. While the clerical lifestyles of these religions appealed to him, liturgical and theological disagreement prevented him from converting. Heartbroken at not finding a path in the ministry, he returned to his home congregation, hoping that by being a part of its faith life and activities he might find a way to Christ. In order to do this he knew he needed to reconcile his sexuality with his faith, but he found spiritual guidance and inspiration appropriate to a gay man nonexistent. Sermons proscribing homosexual behavior, constant reminders of the virtues of marriage and family life, announcements of social events targeting husbands, wives, and their children, and scriptures interpreted in an overly moralistic and literal fashion drained him of any hope of finding a road map for his journey to God in that congregation. One Sunday, looking around the church, he realized there was no one with whom he could identify and no role models upon which he could pattern himself. Furthermore, he did not know of any openly gay person who had achieved both acceptance by the congregation and an internal sense of reconciliation with the Divine.

In order to respond to the Spirit that was still calling him to wholeness, he knew he needed to leave the denomination and life image that had formed a part of his family faith tradition for generations. He grieved for this loss so deeply that it took him a long time before he could explore an alternative path. He knew that to maintain his spiritual integrity he needed a divine affirmation of his goodness, a supportive believing community, and renewed spiritual vision for his future. He eventually found these in the gay Metropolitan Community Church.

Community

James Baldwin once said, "It is a great shock at the age of five or six to find that in a world of Gary Coopers you are the Indian."[7] This feeling of not belonging is a pervasive theme throughout the lesbian and gay experience. All cultures provide their members with a host of shaping stories or life images of the future to help them clarify their identities and their places within that culture. In Judeo-Christian cultures, the stories involving family, vocation, safety, religion, and community are invariably heterosexual in nature

41

and thus provide little guidance or imagery for lesbians and gay men. At some point in their development, people of same-gender orientation realize that they have no place in these stories. This awareness results in the most elemental loss of all, the loss of the illusion that one belongs. This leaves individuals with the feeling of being out of sync with the broader culture and of being an exile in a foreign land, with the attendant losses of status and respectability. Such alienation is played out within the smaller subcultures of which gay and lesbian people wish to be a part but are not. In this section, we will discuss both the subcultural implications of communal loss and the broader cultural elements.

Subcultures. It is a basic human need to belong to and to feel a part of societal groups. These subcultural groups reflect the mythology of the broader culture and are the arenas in which individuals find status and are accorded the respectability that comes with being accepted. Most gay men and lesbians are raised with the image that this is their society too and that membership is as open to them as it is to any citizen. It is with a deep sense of grief that they realize that this image is true for them only if they pretend. They see that prejudice against them is still acceptable in even the most reputable groups of society.

Michael was the all-American boy—handsome, talented, bright, athletic, and the winner of his high school's "most likely to succeed" award. He was also resolutely gay and had known this most of his life. By the time he graduated from high school and entered the military, he had enjoyed intimacy with several boys his age. He appeared so straight that no one in the military suspected his orientation. He had entered the service because it was a childhood dream and because of the status it afforded. He was willing to be discreet about his sexuality in order to secure a career in the military. But within months, he saw numerous incidents of discrimination against those who were only suspected of being gay, a large amount of name calling and innuendo, and some discharges based on only the sexual orientation of those involved. He soon realized that it was only a matter of time before he would receive the boot, so he resigned after his first tour of duty.

Because he experienced a strong need to be part of a team, he looked next to his second choice of occupation, the Catholic priesthood. This pleased his parents deeply and won him wide acceptance and respect from his entire extended family, who threw him a grand party on the eve of his entry into the seminary. He naively imagined that the seminary would provide a more accepting and spiritual home for a person of his orientation than the military and that the grace of God's call would help keep him celibate. Instead, he found a world of secrecy, rumor, and prohibition of anything faintly resembling a "particular friendship."

In the spring semester of his second year, he and Ross fell in love. Even though they were exceedingly careful, their relationship was discovered, and Michael was confronted by the rector with the evidence of his indiscretion. Within hours after the meeting, both his and Ross's parents were called, and the two of them were immediately expelled from the seminary and driven home by their humiliated parents. The details of his dismissal quickly spread through the family, and his folks were shamefaced with embarrassment. Upon arriving at their house, his mother withdrew into her bedroom while his father exploded in rage at Michael's betrayal of their love and trust. He kicked Michael out with these words: "We wanted a priest and a man, not a queer, in this family."

Drawing on his GI benefits, he rented an apartment at a nearby university. Again, his need for belonging and bonding caused him to want to pledge a fraternity. News of his seminary dismissal and rumors of his orientation accompanied him, however, and not a single fraternity granted him an invitation. After only one semester, he realized that most of his old friends who had once voted him "most likely to succeed" were avoiding him, and he subsequently moved to another part of the state to attend college and start his life over.

This syndrome of subcultural rejection and loss of belonging continued after he graduated and tried to settle down with his lifemate, Jonathan. Twice they tried to purchase a home, but both times they reconsidered because they did not want to face the hassles of the neighbors' objecting to their openly gay lifestyle in a family-oriented neighborhood. Similarly, Michael was turned down when he volunteered to be a Boy Scout leader, and Jonathan's application for a men's service organization was refused. Michael ran for a seat on the city council but lost after a campaign filled with slurs and prejudice. On numerous occasions they were excluded from events for couples in their respective jobs. Reluctantly, feeling like exiles, they decided to move to a large urban center for the practicality of finding employment as well as a subcultural community within which they could have greater acceptance and commonality.

The societal life image defines stringent criteria for belonging in our culture; namely, that you and your family members be white, married, middle or upper class, employed, literate, able-bodied, socially appropriate, attractive, slender, youthful, sober, nonabusive, and straight (with straight children, siblings, and parents). Very few people meet these narrow criteria, and when they do, it is generally only for a brief interval in their lives. Gay men and lesbians never fully meet the criteria and thus don't have a complete internal sense of integration with the culture. Deep inside, they always know they are different. They might try to buy into a heterosexually based life image for a while or for a lifetime, but the pervasive sense of being different inevitably returns. Many gay men and lesbians feel so disconnected from their families, communities of origin, or childhood friends that they feel they have no past and that they are exiles from their own history and culture. This awareness of not truly having a life image of one's place in the broader culture and in most subcultural units of society translates into loss.

Broader Culture. Joseph Campbell believes that shaping stories, or myths, help us to understand our passage from birth to death, to find out who we are, to touch the "transcendent," and to discover "the rapture of being alive."[8] The messages conveyed by the overall culture to lesbians and gay men often make them feel as if they were left-handed in a right-handed world and do little to help them formulate life images that take into account the nature of their sexual orientation. The stories also do little to help them embark upon their life journeys, highlight an understanding of their unique calling, or illuminate their inherent

45

connectedness with the Holy; as a result, the stories do little to enhance their "experience of being alive."[9]

Shaping stories and associated images are transmitted to us in a wide variety of ways: from the lips of our grandmothers, as well as through nursery rhymes, popular music, television situation comedies, newspaper articles, billboard advertising, casual conversations, horror movies, romance novels, political campaigns, grammar school textbooks, and nearly every other form of media offering.

To illustrate the pervasiveness of heterosexuality and the scarcity of imagery with which a lesbian or gay person can identify, we will walk through a typical day with Beth. Like many Americans, she starts her morning with coffee and the newspaper. Looking forward to a date with Sylvia that evening, she turns to the restaurant section, only to find a page full of ads picturing families and straight couples. She sighs and moves on to the movie section, trying to find a film that a lesbian couple would enjoy and that is not filled with the angst of heterosexual romance. Having decided on both a restaurant and a movie, she glances through the rest of the paper, taking in the anniversaries, engagements, and wedding announcements. She grimaces at a headline that tells of the murder of a "homosexual" lover and mentally notes that the other crimes reported in the paper fail to indicate the sexual orientation of the people involved.

She leaves for work and turns on the car radio as she drives. Her ears are filled with lyrics of men whose hearts have been broken by the women they love, brokenhearted women jilted by the men they love, girls loving boys, and boys loving girls. She turns off the radio. At work during her morning coffee break, the other women talk about "last night," their upcoming dates, and some details of a spring wedding. Hardly thinking they would care to hear about Sylvia, she contributes nothing. She has a luncheon reunion with a high school chum who prattles on about her husband, her children, and her born-again religion. Again, thinking that any conversation about Sylvia would only occasion prayers for Beth's conversion, she contributes little of substance.

Her work day ends. She walks over to a nationally franchised bookstore to find a gift for a friend with AIDS. After combing through volumes on heterosexual romance, marital problems, the exploits of macho men, boxing, and a health section dealing with every problem imaginable but AIDS, she concludes that, at least for this bookstore, the world of gay men does not exist. She decides to pick up a magazine for herself and is met with a world of women trying to allure men and provide for their culinary, sexual, familial, domestic, and nurturance needs. She leaves the store with a magazine on backpacking for herself and a book on bridge for her friend.

Returning home, she flips through the TV channels as she readies herself for her date with Sylvia. She is treated to a slice of a sermon on the religious channel on the abomination of "homosexual" love, a snippet of news about a court decision denying insurance benefits to gay and lesbian life partners, the "Newlywed Game," the "Dating Game," a political candidate extolling the virtues of the American family, and a talk show on which a popular starlet is describing her recent wedding. She snaps off the TV set and drives over to Sylvia's apartment. She goes inside to greet her, because she knows that the rest of the evening while they are in public, she dare not touch her or in any way give the appearance that she is on a date with her lover.

Beth found herself bombarded by a succession of images that rendered heterosexual reality credible while doing little to help support her lesbian life image. The images that emanated from the experiences of her day, instead of endowing her with a sense of belonging and harmony, assaulted her identity and being in a harshly discordant way. The inability to reconcile her inner world with the outer world in which she lives created a deep feeling of loss, particularly the loss of belonging to the world into which she was born.

Summary

A core element that is common to all the losses described in this chapter is the loss of a feeling of belonging. This sense of not fitting into a hospitable universe deeply affects the attempts of gay men and lesbians to formulate their hopes and plans for the future or, in other words, to develop a life image that will enable them to function from their deepest nature. Without a feeling of belonging, it is virtually impossible to form a life image that is not in some way misshapen, misguided, inappropriate, vague, a set-up for future disillusionment or loss.

But these losses, as anguishing as they appear, are actually necessary for lesbian and gay people, who must lose the illusion that they can assimilate into a heterosexually defined life image. Thus the losses that the individuals encountered in this chapter can be recast as essential birth pangs for the emergence of a more personally viable life image for gay men and lesbians.

In the following chapters we will see how losses can constitute the stepping-stones to spiritual awakening and initiate the deeper process of coming out within.

2

The Path to Transformation

From an early age, many lesbian and gay people feel as though they were not normal, not put together like others. It is their deep sense, as they compare themselves with the images of normality in society, on television, in literature, or in school hallways and locker rooms, that they simply lack whatever it takes to live up to these images. They have trouble generating much energy or interest in pursuits such as dating, sexual exploration, or assimilation into the culturally accepted roles of masculinity or femininity. Lesbian girls and women describe their sheer boredom at the endless female discussions of fingernails, hairdos, and skirt lengths. Gay boys and men tell of their disinterest in masculine bragging about sexual and athletic conquests.

Wanting to be like everyone else, gay and lesbian individuals pretend. They draw around themselves a mask that some writers refer to as a pseudoself or persona. This mask is formed to fit the expectations that others are thought to have. These individuals go all out to assimilate into a heterosexually formed life image, even to the point of becoming homecoming queen, cheerleader, class president, football hero, the star sexual athlete, or in some cases, the best con artist or drug addict. The more intro-verted individuals strive to reach this ideal by trying to please their teachers and obeying their parents, becoming scholars or the most reliable altar boys. In other words, they attempt to adhere to the academic, parental, societal, and religious life images as they perceive them.

The Life Image Defined

Before elaborating on the process involved when an unsuitable societal life image collapses, it is first appropri-ate to discuss further the concept of the life image, or the working model and cherished vision of how individuals expect their lives to proceed. It can be described as a road map for survival, a script for the drama of one's life, or a Life Dream[1] for the future. Life images define how people belong in their environment and reinforce their belief that they do indeed have a place or niche. Because it provides a unifying vision, it also allows individuals to feel a certain sense of mastery or the illusion of control over their destinies. The life image helps people navigate through life, steering clear of their "shadow" emotions of powerlessness and helplessness. A truly viable image enables them to be fully alive, to feel that their core being and vision of their life course are in harmony.

A life image is composed of beliefs and assumptions. Some common assumptions found within most life images include the following: "I trust that the world is a friendly place"; "I can become what I dream"; "My life will be no different from anyone else's"; "I will be treated justly if I do my share"; "We are all important members of the human race"; "With enough effort or work, I can achieve what I set out to do"; and "I can reasonably expect life to turn out as I envision."

At some point in their lives, most lesbians and gay men find that these assumptions do not hold true for them. They encounter homophobia and discover that a significant segment of the world does not desire their presence, that their field of dreams is littered with land mines, and that their orientation makes their lives comparatively different from those of most heterosexuals. They come to see that they are often treated unjustly even when they do their part, that they are not just unimportant to some of their fellow humans but unquestioningly hated, and that some people will actively try to block their efforts at success.

The Loss Process

Some gay and lesbian individuals do not allow these basic assumptions to be challenged to the point that they must redesign their life images. Losses come and go, stopgaps are found, but no attempt is made to reexamine the assumptions underlying the master blueprint of their lives. In spite of the fact that life turns out less and less as they had hoped, the societal life image continues to dominate and direct their existence. The incongruity between the way they had envisioned their life's course and the reality of their outsider status is denied. Many can go on for a lifetime in such a state of dissonance and denial, disconnected from the core self and no closer to the formulation of a more viable life image.

However, when the full impact of the accumulated incongruities strikes home, a loss process can be set in motion. There can be a variety of discrepancies at work in the lives of gay men and lesbians. The most common is the clash between one's private identity and the mask one wears for the public. Another is when there is discordance between who one would like to be and who one is. Many lesbian and gay people would like to be honest and aboveboard but often find themselves sidestepping the truth, hedging, or outright lying lest they jeopardize the place they have in their families, at work, and in society. A third form of disparity (illustrated later in this chapter in the case of Jason) involves the collision between unrealistic life dream assumptions and the harsh reality of life. When any of these three forms of incongruity erupt, the impetus for change can result. As the masklike persona or self-image cracks, or when events dismember the assumptions of the life image, what is exposed is the illusion of the societal life image—namely, that lesbians or gay men can make viable a life image with an exclusively heterosexual focus. The illusion that this blueprint could be their vehicle to being fully alive shatters, leaving them without a road map, without a sense of control, and without a feeling of safety and belonging.

The life image of the broader culture is sunk deeply into the psyches of most people, and losses, like the action of waves, can serve to erode gradually this deep foundation of beliefs and assumptions. After a while or perhaps a lifetime, the nonviable life image is being shored up by fewer and fewer illusions, until one final loss, however small, can topple the edifice. In other words, it may take one last seemingly minor event to bring down what had once seemed to be an indestructible belief system.

In addition to this slow erosion and eventual undoing of an incomplete diagram of life, sudden and devastating loss can also serve as the catalyst for a process potentially leading to the redesigning of a life image. Any of the losses described in chapter 1, whether they relate to family, work, religion, health, or community, can set off a rippling process that either gradually or immediately affects the life image.

The Ripple Effect of Loss

One significant loss can alter the entire life image. In other words, a particular loss snags the fabric of the life image and can lead to the eventual unraveling of the whole garment. The effects of loss, then, impacts the entire being, influencing assumptions about life as well as attachments to these assumptions. Consider the example of Jason.

After a prolonged period of illness, Jason's lover, Bert, died of AIDS. Bert had suffered a great deal, and Jason had faithfully ministered to his needs at home and was at his bedside when he died. Jason and Bert had bonded deeply over their ten years together, and illness had made them even closer. With the loss of Bert, Jason found himself almost incapable of functioning. He felt completely hollow and empty, as though a part of himself had died. It was a struggle to eat, sleep, or concentrate.

During the time of Bert's illness, some of their mutual friends, unable to tolerate the feeling of imminent death that pervaded his home, had begun to drift away. They returned for the funeral, sent flowers to Jason, and then drifted even further away. Invitations for parties and dinner gatherings began to taper off as fewer and fewer of

Jason's social acquaintances felt comfortable enough with his grief to include him. This estrangement worked both ways as Jason found himself becoming increasingly intolerant of conversations about food, movies, and who was doing what with whom when his grief was so great and so many were dying around him.

His relationship with his family shifted with Bert's death as his homophobic mother, barely a week after the funeral, proclaimed him fit to return to the previously inhospitable sanctuary of their Christian home. She explained that this time of grief was his opportunity to repent his "homosexual lifestyle," turn his life over to Jesus, and once again join the company of those who truly loved him. This callous gesture at a time when he most needed unconditional acceptance of his pain and loss only accentuated his sense of alienation from his family and heightened his feelings of aloneness. Now he was not only disconnected from his friends but further estranged from his family as well.

Six months before his death, Bert had resigned from his job, which necessitated Jason's working overtime for his accounting firm. Meeting their mortgage payment as well as the accumulation of medical bills not covered by insurance had depleted their savings. Bert's AIDS diagnosis had so jeopardized his health insurance coverage that the combined medical and funeral expenses left Jason deeply in debt. He was forced to sell the house, move to a small apartment across town, and let go of many of the objects that had been special to Bert and him. Selling their dining room table, around which they had hosted friends and toasted each other, took another piece of Bert from him and left him feeling paralyzed with depression.

The loss of Bert and Bert's things as well as the home they shared together and the move into an unfamiliar setting shattered his sense of security and belonging.

Jason was forced to reveal his orientation at work in order to spend time with Bert during his last days and to make the necessary funeral arrangements. His request for bereavement leave was denied as contrary to company policy. The supervisors he talked to explained that their company supported "family values" and that bereavement leave for a homosexual lover did not qualify as company policy. The depletion of Jason's sick leave and vacation time left him trying to function competently at work while managing the many details of his personal life in the little time that remained. This left him feeling angry and alienated from his company. Exhausted by life, with no time to grieve, he was advised by his doctor to take a disability leave to restore his own health.

Jason had suffered numerous losses. His loss of Bert set into motion a series of losses related to his emotional well-being, friendships, family, finances, residence, job, and health. This, in turn, affected his whole life image, his vision of how he expected life to proceed. As the effects of these losses rippled through his entire being, virtually every assumption incorporated within his life image was challenged.

Like every human, Jason had assumptions about security, predictability, control, protection, belonging, trust, and hope. Bert's death, as would the death of any loved one, compelled Jason to confront the validity of these assumptions in a process that would eventually lead to their revision. Before Bert contracted AIDS, Jason was able to maintain the illusion that he was secure, that his life's

57

course was foreseeable, that their mutual love would enable them to overcome adversity, that his friends, unlike his family, would always be there, and that God was taking care of him. Bert's illness initiated a chain reaction that required Jason to examine the assumptions inherent in his life image. Also caught up in this ripple effect were questions regarding attachments to people, relationships, and even objects such as a home or a table.

Being gay exacerbated Jason's losses and directly challenged many of the assumptions underlying his life image. The pain of loss is similar for all humans, but the nature of Jason's sexual orientation made some of his losses far more difficult than if he had been heterosexual. The dark specter of AIDS in Jason's life and in the community surrounding him, the unconscionable approach of his mother, the injustice meted out by the insurance carriers, and his own company's refusal to respect his need for time to manage his affairs completely destroyed his illusion of being a viable part of the mainstream of society and left him feeling violated.

The Loss Model

Although Jason did not know it at the time, the series of losses that he was experiencing were actually propelling him on a journey toward greater personal and spiritual wholeness. In the next several chapters we will explore in considerable depth the phases of this journey from loss to transformation. Borrowing from John Schneider's model of loss and transformation,[2] we will travel through eight stages, beginning with the shock of an initial loss and culminating with the transformation of a lesbian or gay life image. To give a brief glimpse of this process, we will now accompany Jason through the eight phases.

Initial Awareness. With many major losses, shock is followed by equally severe aftershocks, often making it difficult to determine a starting point. In Jason's case, he experienced shock and numbness when he first became aware of Bert's health status, when Bert was diagnosed with AIDS, and when Bert died. The death itself, however, was the key event that completely disrupted Jason's life.

Holding On. Eventually, out of sheer necessity and partially in the belief that he could overcome Bert's death, Jason threw himself into the work that had piled up at the office. He felt that if he could get some order back into his life and stay busy enough, he could lessen the impact of the loss. He held on to his partner by keeping Bert's clothes as he left them in his closet, sleeping on Bert's side of the bed, and wearing Bert's watch.

Letting Go. Jason experienced a brief phase of trying to devalue or minimize Bert's significance to him when he began to feel resentment toward Bert for leaving him in such a financial mess. He saw himself marshalling a case against Bert and found that the anger kept him from feeling his overwhelming pain. In an act of denial, he threw out all the pictures he had of their last vacation together.

Awareness of Loss. Jason bottomed out. All his efforts to avoid the pain of his loss failed, and he would cry at the least reminder of Bert. He was no longer able to deny that Bert was gone and all that was left was a forgotten sock under the couch. He could barely get out of bed and get through the work day. He often wondered why Bert had died and not he.

Gaining Perspective. After facing the responsibility of selling the house, resettling into his smaller apartment, restructuring his finances, and securing a medical leave, Jason welcomed the time alone. He missed Bert deeply but was not continually aching. He neither expended energy keeping Bert's memory alive nor felt angry at Bert for leaving him behind. Jason felt sad but much more at peace than before.

Integrating Loss. Feeling the need to share his story with others like himself who had lost loved ones to AIDS, Jason joined a survivors' support group. This led to his volunteering with ACT UP, a group designed, among other things, to ensure that people currently struggling with AIDS had access to medications that Bert had not. This public step of integration allowed something to shift inside Jason, and he realized he was emotionally free to move away from Bert. He began dating and chose to paint his apartment blue, a color he wouldn't have chosen while Bert was alive.

Reformulating Loss. Jason left the accounting firm and started his own practice in order to serve a number of full-fee accounts as well as to have the freedom to serve people who were struggling to make ends meet. By means of his volunteer work with people with AIDS, his hope, which had once been so shattered, was restored by the loving kindness of his fellow volunteers and the faith he saw in many of those with AIDS. He reconnected with his mother and felt centered enough to accompany her to church on an occasional Sunday and derive some inspiration from the prayers, music, and fervor of the congregation. He found he could chuckle inwardly at statements by the preacher that would have once infuriated him.

Transforming Loss. Jason came to realize that his period of loss was an experience similar to death. He had virtually died inside and come to life again. This knowledge gave him the courage to open up his heart not only with greater love but also with fewer rules and expectations for his relationships. He came to love Jerry, a doctor at an AIDS hospice. Jason also learned to focus his attention on his mother's good qualities and love for him while allowing her negativity to fade into the background. He and Jerry found that they could worship at a nearby Catholic monastery, where they felt deeply connected to the ancient sights and sounds, the comforting and abiding presence of God, and the stories of faith that provided a vision of hope for the future.

Summary

A life image is a working model of how people expect their lives to proceed. It contains a vision of how to navigate one's passage from birth to death and the assumptions underlying or shaping that journey.

Jason's life image held expectations about when and how death occurs and the way society is to respond to the dying and the bereaved. Throughout his period of loss, it became increasingly more difficult for Jason to hold on to the illusion that the societal life script for grieving persons would hold true for him as well. His denial system shattered when he realized that the work world was often an inhospitable place for a grieving gay man, that a family does not respond to the death of a gay partner as it would to the death of a husband or wife, and that rather than receiving support and sympathy, he received unjust and judgmental treatment. With the destruction of the assumptions that had directed his life, Jason was set on a course leading to the transformation of his losses into a more viable life image.

This chapter has introduced an eight-stage model whereby lesbian and gay individuals can potentially move from the initial awareness of a loss to a more integral and fluid way of viewing events and relationships and existing in the world. The next several chapters will illustrate and describe phases through which the grieving travel toward wholeness.

3

Initial Awareness

Loss is particularly difficult for gay men and lesbians, because the structures of society and the ever-present reality of homophobia can tend to magnify any particular loss as well as increase the sheer numbers of losses, making a difficult recovery process even more difficult. This can give lesbian and gay individuals the impression that life and loss are piling up on them.

People become aware of and react to loss in any number of ways. Loss can come in inches or it can come suddenly with violent impact, but there is some moment when the mind says that a loss is real. At this point, the instinct of humans is to protect themselves from something so threatening as this now-perceived loss. That which is integral to their needs or beings is seen to be gone. They may react with a whole panoply of emotions—disorientation, disbelief, detachment, confusion, numbness, and possibly even full shutdown of all their systems. In the following stories, we will provide examples of how six lesbian and gay individuals reacted to their initial awareness of loss.

Heading Off Awareness

At the urging of his friends, all of whom had been tested, Stewart decided to get a test to determine if he had been exposed to the AIDS virus. He went to a clinic that had been recommended by these friends. After ten days, he returned to find out the results. He sensed that the news might be bad when the counselor ushered him into her office and looked at him with deep concern on her face. When told that his test was positive, his reaction was one of numbness and disbelief. His mind locked onto some of the stories that had been circulating about the potential inaccuracy of an HIV test or a laboratory error due to incompetent or overworked staff or the possibility that his blood was confused with someone else's. He explained to her that he simply did not believe the results, that her lab must have made a mistake, and that he would go elsewhere to be retested. This he did, in fact three times. The results never changed, but Stewart persisted in denying the evidence.

As can be seen in Stewart's case, the initial awareness of loss can be postponed. Rather than confront the reality of the potential loss of his health, he set out on a search for indisputable evidence. Even when the results continued to confirm his positive HIV status, he maintained a stance of disbelief and denied the awareness of an impending loss. His reservations concerning HIV test results were certainly valid, but his subsequent denial in the face of mounting evidence illustrates how people can limit their initial awareness by holding on tightly to what is threatened or engage in other strategies that can delay the shock involved in facing the actual loss.

Breaking Under the Last Straw

Sister Ann had been a nun for seventeen years. She had helped prepare children for their First Communion, couples for marriage, converts for reception into the faith, sponsors for Baptism, and youth for the trials of being adult Catholics. Over the years, she was able to come to terms with her lesbian orientation even to the point of being able to share it with a select circle of friends. She had always comforted herself by thinking that, given that she was celibate and could receive the sacraments of the church, her orientation was not sinful. She had witnessed examples of homophobia in her church but was always able to explain these away by saying, "Prayer can change hearts," "If I don't stay, who will be left to serve God's lesbian and gay people?" or "Christ truly loves homosexuals and the Church will eventually come to see this."

She heard about a lesbians' support group, and she joined it partly out of her own need for community and partly out of a sense that she could minister to the group. Over time her consciousness was raised, and she began to be less comfortable with scriptures that were often misinterpreted as being condemnatory to lesbian and gay people. She found it more difficult to prepare only heterosexual couples for marriage and to teach Catholic doctrine only as it pertained to same-gender relationships. All this incongruity made her less and less capable of maintaining her illusions about her place in the Catholic church. It was increasingly more difficult for her to explain away the discrepancies she was beginning to identify within her belief system.

In November 1986, Sister Ann attended a mass where a guest priest was giving a sermon based on a just-published

Vatican letter entitled "The Pastoral Care of Homosexual Persons." She heard for the first time no distinction made between her celibate status and her lesbian being. She heard her orientation referred to as an "objective disorder" and "an intrinsic moral evil." The priest self-righteously proclaimed that people like herself were a serious threat to the "lives and well-being of families and young people" and that the couplehood of her lesbian friends was "behavior to which no one has any conceivable right."

For the first time, she was unable to deny her illusion that she was a cherished, valuable—much less acceptable—member of the Catholic Church. This event was the indisputable evidence, the last straw, that her life image of functioning within the Church in spiritual harmony and mutual respect was no longer viable. The impact of the preacher's words was like a blow to her body. She was completely shocked and numbed and had barely enough strength to walk out of church.

Both Stewart's case and that of Sister Ann demonstrate a need for indisputable evidence before the reality of an impending loss can be realized. Both existed in a never-never land of disbelief for a considerable length of time. We do not know how long Stewart will deny the reality of his test results, but it took seventeen years of slow erosion before Ann's illusions about herself and her church caved in. She came to see with startling clarity the discordance between reality in all its harshness and the assumptions that had supported her life image. She was devastated as she became aware that her expectations for her church regarding justice, openness, hospitality, respect, and inclusion were deeply violated. That day she truly identified as a lesbian and viscerally knew that the condemnation was directed not to some hypothetical group but to her. This was the indisputable evidence she needed to render the loss real for herself. It was no longer possible for her to limit her awareness by denying discordance, and thus she came face to face with loss.

Being Struck Suddenly

Althea and Lena were a well-known African-American couple who had testified frequently before the city council and planning commission regarding housing discrimination based on the issues of race and sexual orientation. Their articulate and impassioned defense of these causes attracted a fair share of media attention as well as criticism from the Coalition for Family Values. In addition, they had been the target of phone calls and letters from right-wing zealots and religious fanatics.

One evening while they were preparing dinner, Althea had to run to the corner market for pasta and butter needed for the meal. She said that she would be back in ten minutes. Lena became concerned after twenty minutes had elapsed, worried after thirty, and after forty-five minutes went out to look for her. Walking down the sidewalk to the store, she noticed a crowd gathering directly ahead of her. Her worst fear rose in her throat and she ran forward, pushing her way through the people huddled around someone lying on the ground.

Lena knew immediately it was Althea. She had been battered repeatedly and fatally stabbed, and her blouse, face, head, and arms were covered with blood flowing from several wounds. Lena could tell she had tried to protect herself as best she could. She heard the disjointed conversations of eyewitnesses in the crowd telling about men with bats, horrible screaming, a man with a bloody knife stabbing someone, coarse laughter, and words like "die dyke." Lena exploded in rage, losing all sense of composure. Emotions of panic, grief, and terror combined with anger and revenge had her racing about searching for ways to retaliate. Periodically, she broke down in sobs and beat the pavement with her fists. She screamed something about getting a gun to kill the bastards but ended up running in the opposite direction from her apartment. Fearing for her personal safety, several of her neighbors held her until the sheer weight of her grief caused the initial rage to turn to tears of despair.

Unlike Stewart and Sister Ann, Lena had no forewarning of her loss and thus no way to prepare herself for the severity of its impact. The other two tried to use disbelief and denial to minimize their initial awareness. Lena's rage and desire for revenge served this purpose for a brief time, but her degree of trauma was so severe that nothing could keep her from losing her center of balance. As grief, panic, and terror tumbled in one upon the other, she became disoriented and virtually nonfunctional. Suddenly, her life image and all that she held dear were lying crumpled before her eyes. Althea's broken body symbolized to Lena a price paid for speaking out, her lack of safety in society, and the contempt she and Althea had to face to love each other. These impressions came in like rushing waves, leaving her nauseated and immobilized.

Replaying Details

Eli was raised in Utah in the Mormon church. Like all members of his priesthood group, he went on a mission after he graduated from high school. Toward the end of his two-year commitment, he and Hiram were assigned as missionary partners for their work in Puerto Rico. They were constant companions for those months, and, after considerable struggle, they were able to admit their orientation and their love for each other. While on the mission, they were able to maintain their secret, but they feared that when they returned and did not immediately set about to find wives they would be discovered. They arranged to separate, but both planned to find work in Denver within the year, which they did. Both of them worked and attended college while they lived together. They were very careful to keep this arrangement secret—they used different post office boxes and separate phone lines—but gradually suspicions in Eli's family were aroused.

On the pretext of discussing his father's upcoming surgery, Eli was called home to Utah for a family summit. When he walked into the house, he knew something was amiss as conversations abruptly ended and eyes darted in his direction. The Mormon bishop was there along with his parents, his two sisters, and their mates. Each one seemed to have a particular script in the drama of this confrontation. When they were all settled in the living room, the bishop began by bluntly asking if Eli was a homosexual and if he was living in homosexual sin with Hiram. If so, he must forsake Hiram and repent his perversion or face church discipline and excommunication.

His father thanked the bishop and addressed Eli's responsibility as the only male left in his family to continue the family lineage. Next, his mother expressed her love for him, wondered where she had gone wrong, and said she grieved, having asked the Lord to forgive her, for any part she might have played in her son's serious affliction. His sister Elizabeth begged him to repent lest his refusal to do so adversely affect his father's heart surgery set for the coming week—"You have broken your father's heart, Eli." His other sister, Rachel, told of the shame he was bringing upon the family name and how none of them could face the God-fearing people at the ward on Sunday mornings. Rachel's husband chimed in that indeed people were talking about Eli's sinful ways and then confided for the first time how he had overcome his problem with alcohol, adding that Eli could do the same with his perversion. And finally, Elizabeth's husband expounded on the joys of being a family man and how, by Eli's choice of homosexuality, he was missing out on the highest blessings of the church as well as the fullness of God's blessing on his manhood.

The massive assault of familial rejection shut Eli down emotionally. He was so interiorly numb that he sat in his family's living room like a detached observer. As each person spoke, he made a mental recording, which over time he would endlessly replay. It seemed as though his mind was the only part of him that was working, so that when it came time for him to reply, he was speechless. Many minutes of uncomfortable silence hung in the room before he got up and left. He felt like a shell-shocked veteran of combat.

Eli, like Lena, was unable to delay the onset of loss. Its approach was swift and devastating, and while Lena outwardly emoted, Eli shut down everything but his brain. Mentally, he replayed over and over the images and words he had seen and heard in his family home that day. The possible loss of his entire family's acceptance and the rejection by his church was so terrifying that he needed to limit awareness of it and establish some control over his thoughts. The mental rehashing was an attempt to manage the disorientation caused by seven of the most important people in his life delivering seven messages that were discordant with his growing awareness of himself as a gay man with an emerging gay life image. He replayed the video of that day endlessly, almost as if he were trying to get it right. It also would play almost automatically when he closed his eyes in sleep.

Anticipating Grief

Paul and Mel knew that the end was drawing near as what seemed to be an endless series of drug treatments and hospitalizations were having less effect on Mel's AIDS virus. Doctors had told them that Mel had three months at best to live. Mel's virus had not affected his mental functioning, so he clearly understood the distress his lover was currently experiencing and the consequences that Paul would have to face. Each wanted to support the other through their impending crisis. Paul knew Mel wanted to be an active participant in planning the details of his death and funeral. Mel had a strong need not to leave Paul so burdened with logistical details, in addition to grief, that he could not get on with his life. So together they set about to arrange for Mel's passing.

They worked out the particulars of a living will and other details regarding the death itself. Carefully they made out a list of who would be called, and Mel made it clear to Paul that, if at all possible, he wished to die at home. They put their finances in order and drafted a will that gave Paul durable power of attorney. They spent considerable time making the arrangements surrounding the funeral. Together they wrote the obituary and memorial cards; selected the casket, flowers, tombstone, and burial plot; crafted a liturgy that reflected their mutual spirituality; and planned a send-off reception with a select guest list and Mel's favorite foods. They even chose the clothes that they would wear on the day of the funeral.

When death came, Paul felt as if he had been there before. He and Mel had pored over every detail, and Paul had rehearsed each many times in his own mind. From the onset of death through the party at the end, Paul felt emotionally detached from the experience. He mentally checked off the items on the list that he and Mel had so carefully constructed. The anticipation of the death and intricate planning served to minimize Paul's awareness of the magnitude of his loss. Even friends commented at the time of the funeral how well he was handling himself. It was only later when writing thank-you notes that the full impact of his loss hit home.

Unlike the people in the other examples so far presented, Paul was able to anticipate his loss, even to the point of making conscious plans to minimize its impact. By rehearsing the events of Mel's death and funeral and being caught up in completing a well-orchestrated script, Paul delayed his awareness of loss. In our first example, Stewart also delayed his awareness of potential loss; but he employed the strategy of denial to avoid facing reality. Paul was able to confront reality head-on, but in the process he developed a mechanism for controlling the impact of his loss. The mental rehashing of Eli's encounter with his family also served as a means to control and regulate the sheer impact of the initial awareness.

Blocking at the Onset

Marian could remember as if it were yesterday the moment Donna told her she was marrying Perry. They had spent a week together in a friend's cabin in Minnesota and enjoyed the romance of each other's company, swum in the lake during the day, and dined by firelight in the evening. Donna's announcement on the morning of their last day together caught Marian completely by surprise. The week had seemed so right and their bonding so deep that Marian was convinced that Donna loved her. Marian was totally stunned when Donna said that she could not live her life as a lesbian with all the adversities and rejection that such a life could present. She said she wanted to try a "normal" life with a husband and children and made it clear that her decision had nothing to do with Marian. Marian, however, spent the next ten years not believing this and feeling devastatingly hurt, personally rejected, and furious at being deceived by Donna.

Although they never saw each other again, Donna was rarely out of Marian's thoughts. She was so humiliated and ashamed for making a fool of herself with Donna and for believing that Donna loved her that she vowed never to tell anyone her secret. But, while she never openly disclosed it, she kept her secret alive by constantly replaying it again and again in her mind. She rehashed it over and over trying to make sense of it.

One day, ten years after the incident, her Aunt Jane dropped by. Marian had always admired her unmarried aunt's spunk, independence, and earthiness, and had felt her to be a mentor. On this particular day, Jane looked Marian in the eyes, commented on her sadness, and folded her into her arms. The time was right for Marian to talk about her pain. Throughout the entire day and between sobs, she shared her story about Donna. This emotional outpouring allowed her to unblock the awareness of her loss and finally to set her loss process in motion.

The example of Marian demonstrates how one can react in this phase of initial awareness. Had Aunt Jane not sensed that Marian needed to talk that day, Marian could conceivably have gone a lifetime holding this story in her mind, obsessing over its every detail. Given the secrecy and shame that surrounds their orientation, many gay men and lesbians are particularly prone to becoming trapped in this initial phase of grief. By simply being too frightened to trust people and talk about the painful, embarrassing, or what they may consider to be sordid details of their losses, they may block themselves before they have a chance to begin recovering. They may spend years, as did Marian, rehashing a painful secret and thus delaying the onset of the true awareness needed to begin the process that will take them from loss to transformation.

Summary

In each of the six examples in this chapter, some aspect of a person's life image was threatened. The fear of the potential loss involved in this threat activated a denial syndrome that served to limit initial awareness. The way the individuals managed their fear and attempted to prevent the magnitude of pain and loss from overwhelming them constituted either a passageway leading toward wholeness or an end in itself, unwittingly trapping them in this beginning phase.

Life Image. The life image provides a working model for the future, a way for people to belong in their environment, and a road map for life that gives its owners a sense of control over their destinies. The image of himself that was threatened by Stewart's positive test results was that of a man who was sexually attractive and alive, productive and competent at work, respected and accepted by his friends, and possessed of a future. Before it shattered, Ann's life image included a picture of herself as lovingly valuing and being valued by the Catholic church until death and as being a spokesperson for a church that treated all of its members—including gay men and lesbians— in a manner harmonious with the Gospel of Christ. As Ann was bonded to her church, so Lena was bonded to Althea and saw herself securely and lovingly married to her for the duration of a reasonably long life. With Althea's murder, she witnessed the demise of her assumptions about the world being a safe and just place to live for a lesbian woman. With one familial confrontation, Eli lost the hope that his life image would harmoniously connect his future with his past; his hope of remaining linked to and supported by his family and his faith was shattered. In many ways, Paul's lost life dream resembled that of Lena, differing only in the manner in which death terminated his vision of a long life with Mel. Trust was as crucial an element in Marian's life dream as it was in Sister Ann's, both of whom felt violated and betrayed by what they deeply loved. Like Lena and Paul, Marian grieved for a future without the person she had hoped would be her life partner.

Coping Reactions. The illustrations in this chapter also serve to demonstrate some of the more common ways in which individuals react when they initially become aware that their life image is threatened. Stewart and Ann both employed denial, searching for indisputable evidence; Stewart did not even then believe the evidence, and Ann took seventeen years to develop awareness of her actual situation. In contrast, neither Lena nor Eli could deny their losses; the impact of these losses was so sudden and immediate that both sought ways to soften the blow. By giving vent to her rage, Lena at least was doing something. This was in contrast to Eli, who sat in silence, unplugging his emotions and keeping his mind spinning in a fruitless effort to ward off the inevitable loss. Paul's anticipatory grieving kept him as emotionally detached as Eli; they used rehearsing and rehashing to forestall the initial awareness. Marian likewise delayed her grief by endlessly replaying an old event, which did not allow her to vent her emotions or to address the fear generated by the imminent threat to her life dream.

Lessons. The stories in this chapter can teach a great deal about some of the processes involving initial awareness as well as how this phase can be used as a passageway to the eventual reconstructing of the life image. The following are some of the lessons that we see.

1. Some losses by their very nature cannot be postponed forever; they will catch up with you eventually.

2. You can outgrow your ability to deny.

3. Allow yourself permission to emote; at times life takes us apart.

4. Paradoxically, giving in to intense emotion means not that you will be stuck there forever, but just the opposite—not giving in may mean that you will be stuck there forever.

5. The search for the whys and wherefores of a particular loss will take you only so far; until the emotions are also engaged and the loss is felt, the process toward recovery cannot commence.

6. You can rehearse and prepare for a loss, but you still have to pay the piper.

7. To transform loss, you must talk to someone you trust about the events and the emotions involved in the loss.

4

Holding On

Assuming that people have not shut down in the initial awareness phase, they usually engage in one of two kinds of coping processes holding on or letting go. The now-acknowledged loss is perceived as a threat against which protection must be mobilized. Quite understandably, people are afraid to lose what is important to them and thus will try to buffer themselves however possible from the magnitude of loss. This chapter will illustrate ways in which gay men and lesbians often attempt to hold on to what they cherish in order to resist the dismantling of their life images and to guard themselves against the suffering that loss will inevitably bring. Chapter 5 will discuss other buffering strategies, known as letting go, which are ways to reduce pain by quickly separating oneself from the loss and which can be engaged in concurrently with, before, or after holding-on strategies.

The human organism can absorb only so much trauma at once without serious consequences and does its best to protect itself by throwing up filters that will gradually regulate the input of emotions and thoughts, allowing only a certain amount to be assimilated at once. In this process of regulating, people may feel as though they were losing their minds, behaving foolishly, or not acting like themselves; in fact they are probably doing exactly what they need to be doing to nurture themselves, maintain their sanity, and keep themselves from becoming overwhelmed by grief.

If one has a certain level of awareness of this, holding-on behaviors will probably be temporary. However, if these behaviors are relied on too heavily and unconsciously become a primary way of functioning in the world, a modus operandi, then the individual risks getting stuck at this point and may never address the true nature of his or her loss. The following six stories will illustrate behaviors that are somewhat nonfacilitative of grieving and could tend to extend reliance on holding-on strategies, thus leaving these people's personalities in suspended animation. Subsequent chapters will show individuals whose use of holding-on strategies has facilitated their passage through grief to subsequent phases of loss.

Running Fast in Place

When people spoke about Andrew, they invariably described him as the most hardworking, kind-hearted human being they had ever met. On the other hand, Andrew, whenever he would allow himself time, thought of himself as the bearer of a shameful secret and possessed of a longing that he dare not satisfy. His work had kept these thoughts and feelings at bay for years. Now, at age forty-three, he was the top social worker in his unit by day and a wizard at the bridge table by night. Andrew was chosen by his department to attend a five-day conference in Atlanta; this trip would be his first departure from his hometown in twenty years. The very thing he had been most fearfully avoiding all those years happened at the conference—he met a man and had sex for the first time in his life. His terror at the possibility of acknowledging his homosexuality and its ramifications for his life image literally propelled him out of the hotel at dawn and on to the first available plane home. He never did stop running. Andrew threw himself headlong into his work and community endeavors, compulsively adding to his already formidable caseload and volunteer activities. The need to be seen as competent, which had driven him all his life, began driving him even harder. Even more people came to describe Andrew as the most hardworking, kind-hearted man they had ever met.

As a result of his encounter with the man at the conference, Andrew was in grave danger of losing his illusions that a heterosexually formed life image was a viable fit for him. Acknowledging the real nature of his sexual orientation would have required him to challenge the assumptions that were shoring up his life vision. By compulsively holding on to the status quo, he was able to limit any further awareness of this loss. The praise he received from working hard had over time become his only reward system, so he could ill afford to challenge the assumptions underlying his workaholism. He was afraid not to believe that he could outrun this threat, and he continued believing that his hard work could overcome anything. By running as hard as he could, devoting himself to causes, and focusing his attention outside of himself, Andrew was able to hold on to his life image and thus diminish the full impact of his loss.

Bargaining and Being Good

Caroline could not remember ever having felt very sexual, even though she had been married to Roy for ten years and had given birth to two daughters. Her lack of passion and response had disturbed Roy to the point that he had begun bringing home pornographic videos showing male and female couples as well as an occasional one of two women engaged in sexual behavior. Initially she was disgusted, but something was compelling her to continue watching. She became sexually aroused watching the women and found herself assuming the role and feelings of each female actress. When it dawned on her how much she wanted to be with a woman, it horrified her. She sought out the help of her minister, who convinced her of the evils of homosexual feelings and the depravity of pornography and prayed with her to denounce these demonic influences and turn her life over to Jesus.

For Caroline, the threat of losing her life image as a wife, mother, and good Christian woman was imminent. She knew she had to bargain for her very soul. She was willing to do anything to prevent her illusions about being a God-fearing woman with "family values" from being challenged. If the Lord would release her from her homosexual affliction, she would work tirelessly in his vineyard, organizing pickets at the local X-rated video store. In addition to this crusade against the evils of Satan, she brought her ever-present born-again smile to numerous church gatherings to speak about a Christian's responsibility to turn homosexuals from their sinful paths.

Much like Andrew's, Caroline's potential loss involved the assumptions and illusions contained in her societal and religious life image. The pleasurable emotions she experienced as she watched her husband's videos so terrified her with their implications that she became willing to promise anything to be free of them. Perpetual bargaining in the form of rigid niceness and religious crusades constituted her way of defending against loss. By enlisting God's help in eradicating her sexual feelings, she was able to contain the menacing threat and thus hold on to her life image.

Narrowing One's World

Jim was born in 1932 and was an only child. He lived with his family in a small town in central California. He was a loner, but he came to life in high school in the world of drama and acting. Here was a forum where he could express himself and be affirmed. In the spring semester of his senior year, he fell in love with Lyle, another drama student. Word of that relationship leaked out, and while he was acting in the last play of the school year, he saw several students mouthing the word "queer" until it became an audible chant in the auditorium. This incident caused the principal to call him before the administration, where he was accused of "abominable acts and perversion" with Lyle. He was allowed to finish the last few weeks of school but forbidden to act in the play or to see Lyle. He never spoke to Lyle again, completed school, and left town without even attending his graduation ceremony.

While waiting tables in Los Angeles, he was befriended by Daniel, an older professional man. He moved into Daniel's home and remained there for two years as

Daniel's lover. The climate in Los Angeles was repressive for gay men and lesbians in the early fifties, and the two of them kept pretty much to themselves and took few chances to be exposed publicly. Given the pain he had suffered in his relationship with Lyle, Jim was unwilling to upset Daniel in any way for fear of another upheaval and rejection that would leave him out on the street. For all his efforts to avoid conflict, one day he returned home from the restaurant to find his belongings on the front porch with a note saying, "So long, kid, I'm tired of you," signed Daniel.

With two relationships dissolving one right after the other, Jim felt terribly rejected. Quite understandably, his life image reflected his need for acceptability, respect, and security. Daniel's eviction of Jim from his life was the last straw, threatening Jim's self-image, feeling of control, and sense of the continuity of his life. Out of fear, he set about creating a world that, though it was artificial, was predictable and safe, and allowed him a role in which he would be needed and respected.

Eventually, he found a job as an attendant at a mortuary with an apartment upstairs provided for him as part of his salary. He never moved from that apartment. Over the years, he was promoted in the mortuary to being the assistant to the owner, planning the services, and making arrangements with grief-stricken families.

Jim gloried in the role, dressing each day in his immaculate pin-striped suit, cuff-linked shirt, and glossy black shoes. He was sought after for his helpfulness and discretion and proved equal to any problem a bereaved patron might direct his way. Jim came to see that God had a purpose for him when he removed Lyle and Daniel from his life. Given that he had such noble work to do, he reasoned that God wanted him to devote himself heart and soul to meeting the needs of others in their time of sorrow. Thus he had no friends and habitually took his meals alone at the neighborhood restaurant where he had once served as a busboy.

The potential loss of acceptability, respect, and love threatened Jim's life image. His fear of this loss was so great that he set about creating a world in which he would feel valued, needed, and important without all the uncertainty that his personal relationships had brought. Thus, in order to hold on to what was crucial to his life image and identity, he narrowed his world into one that was orderly, safe, and predictable. By ritualizing his human contacts and making sacred his mortuary duties, he deluded himself into thinking that he was a minister to all and close friend to none.

With the eviction by Daniel, Jim was confronted with yet a second rejection. Rather than acknowledging his helplessness and his need to grieve over the loss, however, he chose to view it as a threat to be overcome and a problem to be solved. His solution was to narrow his world, establish an illusion of control and respectability, and thus prop up his shaky life image. Like Caroline and Andrew, he created a world in which he was able to gain respect, keep illusions intact, and maintain a lid on his fear and potential grief. Whereas Andrew became a compulsive workaholic and Caroline a closeted crusader, Jim emerged as a role-bound public servant. One can only wonder what they might have developed into had they allowed their loss processes to unfold into transformative experiences.

Blaming as Distraction

Martha and Cindy had been lovers for seven years. Over the past year, Cindy had been acting emotionally withdrawn from Martha, who chose to overlook this. On a Friday night, after being away on a week's buying trip for her department store, Martha came home to find Cindy's things gone and a note on the kitchen table. In it Cindy explained that she was no longer in love with Martha and that she was moving in with Tracy, with whom she was deeply in love.

Martha went to pieces. The love of her life had been taken from her, and someone besides herself was going to pay. Rather than give in to her feelings of loss, she plotted revenge. She found herself obsessed with the thought of Tracy in bed with Cindy and said to herself over and over again, "Cindy is mine, she doesn't belong to that other bitch." Her jealousy drove her to discover their address, their unlisted phone number, the kind of car Tracy owned, and where she worked. Thus informed, she set about making them suffer as grievously as she had. Martha called them at night when she thought they might be making love, wrote letters to their mutual friends telling about Cindy's mistreatment of her, called Tracy's boss and informed him that his employee was lesbian, told Cindy's dying mother the same thing, and broke into their home and torched their bed. Finally, Cindy and Tracy ran out of patience as well as legal options and decided to move out of town to avoid further harassment.

Martha started out to win in her battle for revenge against Cindy and Tracy but ended up the loser. Rather than accepting the grief and helplessness of her loss, Martha chose to blame her ex-lover and the other woman for her suffering and thus ensured that they suffered to the degree that she had. All her obsessing and acting out merely served to distract her from her own loss but did nothing to bring Cindy back to her. While it succeeded somewhat in reducing her helplessness, reinforcing her illusion of control, and limiting the awareness of the magnitude of her loss, Martha's holding on so tightly to Cindy and to resentment prevented her from moving through grief and progressing toward a restored life dream.

Wishing It Away

Janet had fought hard for custody of Mindy, her three-year-old daughter. Her ex-husband had employed expensive lawyers and expert witnesses to show that her lesbianism made her an unfit mother. Through the help of a lesbian and gay legal association, she had won her case and was overjoyed to have Mindy back with her in Florida. Several months after the trial, she joined some friends at a luncheon and entrusted Mindy to the care of a babysitter who was hired for the day.

The facts were sketchy on what happened, but Janet remembered the babysitter running into the living room, yelling hysterically, "Mindy's on the bottom of the pool," and repeating those words over and over again. Everyone ran to the pool and several dove in and brought Mindy's lifeless body to the edge. Someone called an emergency number while Janet tried cardiopulmonary resuscitation, but to no avail. Mindy was dead. Everyone was amazed that Janet, given her closeness to Mindy, was able to provide instructions on what to do next. She calmly asked for a blanket to cover the body, gave the name of a funeral home to the ambulance attendant, and told someone to notify the child's father. She then proceeded to ask the sitter about the details of the drowning and about how Mindy had separated herself from the group of children while they were playing tag.

The full impact of the loss hit her over the next few weeks as she lived among Mindy's things. She became preoccupied with her need to understand every detail of Mindy's death. She found herself starting many sentences with "if only … " (if only I had watched her myself, if only I had not left her with the babysitter, if only I hadn't gone to that luncheon, if only I had taught her to swim when I got custody of her). She felt there was a key to understanding this tragedy; all she needed to do was find it and maybe she could undo Mindy's death. Nonetheless, all this searching for the missing puzzle piece didn't buffer her from her grief.

Not being able to wish it away, she decided to have another baby. She and her lover, Ellen, had talked about artificial insemination even before Mindy's death, and several of their friends who were in couples were the recent proud parents of baby boys. After several visits to the insemination clinic, Janet became pregnant.

She and Ellen rejoiced when Philip was born, and they loved him deeply. As time went on, however, Janet continued to miss Mindy intensely and realized that her wishing and her substituting of Philip couldn't protect her from entering into the full extent of her loss.

Janet's intense searching for answers and continual replaying of "if only" scenarios represented not only a way to keep Mindy alive but also a means to deal with her own guilt. People in the holding-on phase often experience an unreal or heightened sense of personal responsibility—that somehow they caused the loss and if they search long and hard enough they might reverse it.

After spending every cent she had to prove that she was fit to be Mindy's mother, Janet's guilt at not being able to protect her child and keep her alive was overwhelming. She would do anything to have her baby returned, to turn the clock back in time. Even giving birth to another child was, at some level, a way to restore Mindy to life. Like the other individuals in this chapter, Janet was attempting to shore up her faltering life image, which had been damaged first by the custody battle and then by Mindy's drowning. As a lesbian mother, she was particularly sensitive to society's judgment and had felt a need to try harder to create a viable family for herself, Ellen, and Mindy. She held on because she was so fearful of the pain of losing not only Mindy but also what Mindy represented for her dreams and her life image.

Pining for the Good Old Days

Gary longed for the days before AIDS had decimated his community. He felt particularly overwhelmed at Ray's funeral when it struck him that he himself was the last survivor of the group of six who had made a yearly summer pilgrimage to a rented beach house. They had started the tradition back in 1976 when they had graduated from college. Then the gay world had seemed bright and open, and the six of them could overcome any obstacle, whether it was homophobia or a hangnail. His friends were so beautiful then, so healthy and tanned and graceful. He remembered their nights of celebration and days of volleyball and swimming. Gary knew he'd never find friends like this nor would there ever again be a time when gay men could be so innocent and so outrageous. The times had been perfect, but now they were over forever.

Preoccupied with thoughts of former days and incapable of seeing anything but loneliness and death in his future, he gave in to despair. His days were filled with memories that continued to replay throughout the nights, both awakening him and keeping him from sleeping. Insomnia started to take its toll on his body, and he complained of constant aching and exhaustion. He felt that the only way to keep his friends and the old days alive was by concentrating on each memory and holding on to the minutiae of their every moment together.

The loss of what Gary considered to be his five closest friends, as well as other people in his friendship network, was a massive assault to his being. He needed to do everything possible to protect himself from being overwhelmed. Coming out for Gary had been fraught with rejection and condemnation, and these five friends had provided him with the security and acceptance he so desperately needed. He built his life image around them; they and the newly liberated gay world became his family and community. Their deaths so destroyed his life image that he had no blueprint for either the present or the future. On some level, he was aware that for a considerable time after their deaths he would not be able to engage fully in the real world and that life for him had to exist only in the past. He needed to limit his awareness lest the power of his trauma drive him to the brink of insanity. He felt he had to hold on to the past in order to keep his hold on reality.

Summary

Once initial shock has registered, people move to protect themselves from its full impact. Some action is taken until the loss can be integrated into the rest of life. The losses you have seen in this chapter were so traumatic that the individuals could easily have been emotionally overwhelmed had they not acted to limit awareness of the magnitude of their loss. In each case, their life images were in some way threatened and they desperately held on to what was in danger of being lost.

Life Image. The life images of our first three examples, Andrew, Caroline, and Jim, are largely societal in their focus, while those of the latter three, Martha, Janet, and Gary, are more relational in nature. Andrew had selected the mental self-portrait of a respectable, hardworking, heterosexual pillar of the community. Respectability was also an integral element in the pictures Caroline and Jim had of themselves, the former seeing herself as a righteous, Christian, family woman and the latter as a man who was publicly revered and possessed of a mission. The life images of Martha, Janet, and Gary revolved around specific individuals—Martha's around Cindy, Janet's around Mindy and Ellen, and Gary's around his five friends. Each had a vision of her or his life and the place and permanence of certain loved ones in this scenario. Martha's image of herself was one of the lover and the beloved, Janet's was of the against-all-odds perfect lesbian family, and Gary's was of the secure community of friends-for-life.

All six individuals had mapped out fairly concrete, inflexible life images. Because Andrew, Caroline, and Jim had images that were heavily reinforced by other people, they became more rigid when loss struck. In fact, one wonders if the holding-on strategies adopted by these three in their times of crisis became permanent patterns that kept them from ever successfully grieving over their losses.

Insofar as the losses of Martha, Janet, and Gary clearly and observably snapped their unbendable life images, they were simply not able, as were the first three, either to deny their losses or to gain reinforcement from others for maintaining their old life images. In fact, because their losses were so public, there was little chance for them or others to pretend that they had never happened. Because the losses of Andrew, Caroline, and Jim were much more private and symbolic, they were able to ignore their losses and thus hold on, possibly for a lifetime, to their non-viable life images.

Coping Reactions. To buffer the threats to their images, each of the individuals in this chapter used a number of coping devices. Three of them attempted to enshrine others in order to hold on to a crumbling life dream. Gary made his friends bigger than life since he felt as if they were all he had. Martha convinced herself that she simply couldn't live without Cindy, and Janet had invested her self-image as a mother and a worthwhile person in her daughter Mindy.

Assuming a role was another means to keep the hounds of reality at bay for Caroline, Andrew, and Jim. But the most common form of coping with reality was by acting out. Caroline became an unrelenting crusader for the forces of good against evil. Martha employed blaming to keep her life image from self-destructing, and Janet conceived Philip to do the same. Andrew, to keep his image propped up, never quit running from himself and his sexuality. Finally, Jim and Gary acted out by creating worlds of their own, one filled with illusions and the other with ghosts.

Lessons. The stage of holding on is inevitable for individuals passing through loss. It is understandable that people will reach out and grab for the debris of their shattered life dreams. And by this same token, it is a phase in which many can get stuck—sometimes for the rest of their lives and sometimes until the next significant loss comes and forces an uprooting of their nonviable life images. The following lessons are given to help avoid these consequences and to facilitate passage through this stage.

1. If you are aware that your way of holding on is a strategy to limit awareness, it is probably facilitative of grieving; if you are unaware, it is probably not.

2. Often, holding on is a protection for a broken heart. Only hearts that can love deeply can be broken; be grateful for this.

3. Losses that are not shared are often blocked in the holding-on phase.

4. You cannot run away from yourself—you always take yourself with you.

5. You can always choose to build your life around your secrets and others may praise you for it. That still does not make it right.

6. With public losses, there are often helping hands to pull you along; with private, symbolic ones, you are often alone . . . if you choose.

7. Making memories your only reality cannot replace living in the present and embracing a future.

5

Letting Go

When the initial awareness of loss hits home, people often embark on a set of responses that interweave holding-on with letting-go strategies. As we have seen, holding on involves beliefs and behaviors that attempt to maintain the status quo of a life dream. With letting go, individuals acknowledge their losses but indulge in activities and thinking that dismiss the significance of the lost life image. Like holding-on efforts, letting-go behaviors protect people from being overcome by the magnitude of their losses and help them manage the pain of losing something or someone that was once cherished. Letting go is a strategy of separating that which was once valued from the self. Individuals in this stage might say, "If it's not a part of me, it can't hurt me," "He (she or it) wasn't important anyway," or "To hell with it (him or her)."

Use of behaviors such as these is a natural part of living and coping with losses, even the most minor ones. But in losses that directly threaten the life image, letting-go strategies can be even more pronounced. We will encapsulate some of the more poignant dynamics of this phase in the following six case examples. While most lesbians and gay men will be able to navigate through the letting-go stage, our focus will be on those who are in danger of excessive reliance on letting-go behaviors and who, thus, may remain stuck in this stage. Again, individuals who make more facilitative passages will be illustrated in subsequent chapters.

Five out of six examples will exemplify people who are clearly in the letting-go stage of loss. The first example, however, demonstrates a common tendency of individuals to alternate between holding-on and letting-go strategies. When these two processes are used in tandem, people often find themselves emotionally alternating from disgust to guilt and from deification to denigration. At one moment they are savoring memories, and at the next they are cleaning out their psychic closets.

Swinging Between Phases

Seth was surprised to hear his mother's voice on the phone, since he hadn't talked with his parents for two years. She said, "Seth, please come home. Your father has had a heart attack and may not live long. He wants to see you." Seth took the next plane from Houston to Omaha and found his father, Henry, lucid but in critical condition. When Seth walked into the room, tears came into Henry's eyes, and he raised his arms in a feeble gesture of welcome. Seth sensed that his dad wanted to be held, and he bent down, embraced Henry, and let himself be kissed on the forehead. In a barely audible voice, Henry told Seth that he never felt right about throwing him out of the house two years ago. He wanted Seth to know how much he loved him and how much he desired his son's forgiveness.

As much as Seth wanted to accept his father's apology and set matters right between them, he felt considerable internal conflict. He heard himself mumbling words of assurance, love, and forgiveness, but inside he could still hear the old tape of his father's anger: "No fag is going to live in my house," and "If you want to live like a queer, you'll have to do it somewhere else." That night his father died.

To deal with his father's death, Seth found himself alternating between moments of intense nostalgia about their good times together and times of wanting to curse Henry's memory. Some days he wore his father's old ties and desperately wished he were alive again so they could continue the mending of their relationship that had begun on Henry's deathbed. Other times, Seth found himself raging to friends about the "abusive, homophobic old bastard" and all the pain that his father had caused him. He felt himself alternately torn between disgust and guilt, acceptance and rejection, love and hate. His ambivalence caused him to hold on to Henry's memory by sending money to the heart fund, and shortly thereafter to let go of Henry by ripping out his picture from its frame and burning it in the wastebasket. These pulls continued until he literally ached inside and decided to seek professional help.

Henry's deathbed apology resurrected for Seth a childhood life image of acceptability: he saw himself as a cherished son of a loving father and a valued member of his family. This last conversation with his father brought to the surface a dream whose demise he had begun to mourn two years earlier when Henry had evicted him from his home. Having had only a fleeting taste of his lifelong wish for Henry's respect and for his place in the family as a gay man, with no opportunity to truly experience these realities in everyday living, was a deep loss for Seth. The life image he so desperately desired was his for but a moment. In order to protect himself from the pain of wanting something he could now never have, he needed to remind himself of how cruel his father had been to him. The brief attempt at reconciliation was not substantial enough to allow Seth to resolve his already ambivalent feelings; thus, after Henry's death, the ambivalence continued.

Dropping Out of Life

At an early age, Connie experienced herself as different from other girls, with interests and feelings unlike those of her peers. Although she was unable to express it until much later in life, she sensed that her attraction toward other girls was different from theirs toward her. She further intuited that this was something she dare not talk about. This guardedness usually took one of two forms: an endless chatter that skirted anything remotely connected to her true orientation or withdrawal into silence for fear that any information about her shameful secret would leak out.

In high school, she became attracted to Glenda, her best friend. They spent a great deal of time together, shopping, going to movies, and spending the night at each other's houses. Once when they were lying on the bed talking, Connie reached over, put her arms around Glenda, and tried to kiss her. This terrified and confused Glenda, who pushed Connie away and said, "You're not one of *them,* are you?"

Connie reacted by saying, "Oh, no, I'm not and I won't touch you ever again."

Connie wasn't able to recover from what she perceived as Glenda's rejection of her and, in fact, never touched anyone for fear of it happening a second time. She pulled back from Glenda and eventually from society in general. She briefly took a nine-to-five job working on an assembly line but quit in her early twenties after the death of her father. She reasoned that since her mother was alone, she needed company. Due to her own dependency needs, Connie's mother supported her logic as well as her lifestyle. Connie barely ventured out of her mother's home. She would spend her time snacking, retreating into fantasy by watching television and videos, putting jigsaw puzzles together, and playing computer games. She came to trust almost no one. In fact, she did her marketing late at night in order to encounter fewer people. When she did leave the house, she was continually vigilant for fear someone might assume she was homosexual and assault her. She also reasoned that if she put on enough weight, she would be protected from harm.

The tendency to see the world in dichotomous terms is prevalent in most letting-go processes. Connie is a good example of this. When her life image of connecting with and belonging to another woman was shattered, she reacted by separating herself from any vestige of this image. She never attempted attaching herself to another human being other than her mother. If she couldn't trust one person, she wouldn't trust anyone. If she couldn't be attractive to Glenda, she wouldn't be attractive to any other person.

If reality was too painful, she would live in fantasy. If the world was dangerous, she would create one that was safe.

She lived in a world of split reality with definite good and bad, black and white, in which it was me versus them. Central to her life image was to love and to be loved by another human being. With this denied her, she let go of any further attempts to fulfill her dreams and escaped from life.

Burning Bridges

When Jean was growing up, she knew that no one else felt about other women as she did. She succeeded in suppressing her feelings even to the extent of finding a long-distance truck driver to marry her. On hindsight, she realized what most attracted her to Sam were his frequent absences from home and his habit of sleeping much and demanding little when he was home. She was lonely most of the time and she knew it wasn't because she longed for Sam. There was a part of her that she shared with no one.

Jean didn't seem to fit anywhere, particularly with the other wives who gathered at the end of the afternoon for a few drinks before their husbands arrived home. She soon realized her motivation for mixing with this group was different from that of the others and that a strange attraction was growing within her toward one of the women there. One day, Sam came home and snickered about being out on Highway 93 and accidentally stumbling into a "dyke" bar. She made a mental note that the next time he was out of town, she was going to check it out.

The following week, Jean entered her first lesbian bar, and it felt like a homecoming. She instantly felt as though she belonged there, surrounded for the first time in her life by a group of women like herself. The semi-darkness, the air filled with cigarette smoke, the rock music, and the laughter of the other women cast a trance-like spell that was to call her back again and again. It was only here, she decided, that she could relax and be with other "outcasts" like herself.

Eventually, Jean divorced Sam and began to spend almost all of her free time in the bar, where she was known for her earthy advice and capacity to make others feel at home. Over time, though, her newfound friends became concerned by her excessive drinking. Four of them put their heads together and discussed what to do with her. They agreed that she had to be confronted by all of them together and encouraged to go to an alcohol treatment center that worked well with lesbians.

Jean was shocked and didn't seem to hear their mes-sage. Rather than hearing that they loved her and wanted her to recover and still be their friend, she heard that they judged and rejected her and wanted to get rid of her. She was incensed and told them all to get lost and to get out of her life forever. She even returned to the bar on the next Saturday night, stood up on the piano, and shouted above the din, "F– off, you bitches. You'll never see me again." And she moved far away, to Cincinnati. From time to time, she felt intense guilt and remorse over rejecting her friends, but she was too ashamed to face them and effect a reconciliation.

Studies have shown that approximately 30 percent of the lesbian and gay male population have experienced problems with alcohol, compared with a much lower percentage of heterosexuals.[1] Due to societal homophobia and oppression, bars have constituted one of the only known places for gay men and lesbians such as Jean to gather in safety, be affirmed, and socialize. Also contributing to the high rate of chemical dependence among people of same-gender orientation is the need felt by some to relax the vigilance with which they protect themselves. The taking of drugs and alcohol succeeds in lowering the inhibitions resulting from their constant guardedness. Likewise, it can initially help bridge the distance that some lesbians and gays keep between themselves and others. Unfortunately for Jean, alcohol destroyed the bridges to friendship and belonging that it had once served to construct.

With the intervention of her friends, Jean perceived her life image of belonging and being an accepted part of a community to be shattered. The alcoholism had advanced to such an extent that she couldn't recognize that they were rejecting it and not her. Letting go of relationships and burning emotional bridges were Jean's ways of denying her problem and protecting herself from what she alcoholically perceived as the loss of her life image. Like Connie, Jean engaged in dichotomous thinking and completely severed herself from any reminders of what she once felt was integral to her vision of happiness.

Accentuating the Negative

Peter had been very involved in his Catholic parish and was justifiably proud of his contributions to it over the years. He was elected by other parishioners to be a member of the parish council and was selected by Father

Kraus to sit on the five-person finance committee. Utilizing his background in scripture, he served as a lector and enthusiastically proclaimed the stories of faith each Sunday.

Peter's sexual orientation was no secret to most members of the parish. He and his lover Artie were careful not to call attention to themselves and were as welcomed to social affairs as were heterosexual couples. People genuinely liked them and respected their relationship. Father Kraus was particularly supportive of Peter and often sought his advice. In fact, Peter was one of the first people he told when he decided to leave the priesthood.

Father Waters was sent by his bishop to replace Father Kraus and was given the instruction to "clean up the parish" and restore it to orthodoxy. Among his first targets were the gay men and lesbians, especially those like Peter and Artie, whose lifestyle, according to Father Waters, "defied the clear and consistent teaching of the church as regards homosexuality." With a phone call, Father Waters informed Peter that his services as a lector and as a member of the parish council and finance committee were no longer in the best interest of the Catholic church.

At first, Peter was stunned. Then he tried to reason with Father Waters, but to no avail. He next began to tell himself that this was probably for the best, that he had become overcommitted and was growing weary. But this line of reasoning worked only for a while as he found himself growing more cynical and angry. He told Artie he didn't give a damn about the Church anyway since it catered only to straights and officially condemned people in committed relationships like themselves. Peter continued to build a case against the value of the Catholic church in his life, saying he must have been blind all those years and proclaiming himself "a recovering Catholic."

In the letting-go phase, it is common to denigrate aspects of the threatened life image. All the individuals we have seen thus far in this chapter accentuated the negative elements of what they once valued. Seth downplayed his father's importance to him, Connie belittled her need for human companionship, Jean convinced herself that her lesbian friends didn't matter to her, and Peter dismissed the Church's relevance in his life. Before severing ties, they all painted with a black brush their former life images, thus making their letting go of them seem that much easier. Seth, Connie, and Jean all reduced the significance of people, but Peter's case demonstrates that the process of letting go can also apply to organizations, as well as to symbols and inanimate objects.

Devaluing the Self

Larry was a delicate child due to an early history of illness. Having to protect his fragile health in his formative years, he never developed much in the way of athletic abilities or interests. He remembered the other guys in junior high school ridiculing him for what they considered his effeminate manner. Even though he desperately wanted to be a member of the team, he became the focus of their taunting, enduring such names as "Fag" and "Fairy Larry." He was consistently hazed by his classmates and coaches, both on the playing field and in the locker room. As his awareness that he was gay increased, his sense of shame and humiliation intensified to such a degree that he came to see himself and his body as contaminated and worthless.

Feeling so worthless and devalued, at age twenty Larry began using drugs to create highs and involving himself with an almost endless variety of sexual partners. For the first time in his life, he felt masculine and attractive in the eyes of others. Having heard "Fairy Larry" shouted at him so often, he desperately craved the affirmation that was now being accorded him. Even though his better judgment told him that "messing around" wasn't good for him, his intense need for validation of his devalued self prevented him from stopping. Only when he developed antibodies to the AIDS virus and joined a support group was he able to begin affirming himself in a more positive manner.

Like most young men of his age, Larry had been conditioned by society to desire a life image of masculinity and attractiveness. When that proved unavailable to him on heterosexual terms, he let go in much the same way as the other characters in this chapter—he dichotomized. If he couldn't get what he wanted their way, he would do it on his own terms.

The loss of their life images affects the way many gay men and lesbians relate to themselves physically. Having so absorbed the shame directed to them by society, they sometimes shame their bodies accordingly. Larry and Connie both disavowed their physical beings symbolically by cutting themselves off from the neck down. Having felt themselves debased by society, they treated themselves likewise. Larry, like many gay men before the advent of

AIDS, used sex as a way to bring his objectified self to life and to restore a semblance, however bogus and destructive, of a lost life dream.

Rejecting Life

Eileen was serving as a high school principal when Margaret, her lover of ten years, was killed suddenly in a car wreck. They had been very close and had managed to keep their relationship extremely private lest anyone in their small Iowa town find out. Margaret was a successful lawyer, and the impression they projected was of two professional women who chose to purchase a house together. Eileen's usual strict, efficient, and businesslike manner crumbled as a result of Margaret's death. Up to this point, she had relied solely on Margaret to meet her emotional needs, but now she desperately needed to share her grief with someone. She turned to Grace, a fellow principal whom she had known for many years and who had proven trustworthy in professional matters in the past.

Eileen had no way of knowing that five years earlier, Grace had been a candidate for Eileen's job and that since then she had been harboring a grudge for what she felt was an unjust appointment. This was the chance she had been looking for. Confident that she would get Eileen's job, Grace decided to force Eileen to resign by threatening to expose her. Over the phone, Grace explained that she felt Eileen was emotionally and morally unsuited for her position as principal. Furthermore, if Eileen chose not to resign, then Grace would feel compelled to expose her relationship with Margaret to the school board, the PTA, and the local newspaper.

This phone call immobilized Eileen, and in her grief-stricken state, she was unable to think clearly or seek further advice for fear her trust would again be betrayed. Fear of public humiliation, exposure as a lesbian, loss of reputation, and possible loss of her life work overwhelmed Eileen and left her feeling that suicide was her only way out. That night she closed the garage door, connected a hose to her car's exhaust pipe, sat in the car, and turned on the ignition. Neighbors discovered her body the next morning.

Eileen was dealing with many losses at once, all of which affected her life image. Up to this point, she had seen herself as a respected, contributing member of her community, as a woman with an excellent reputation as a school administrator, and as the life partner of Margaret. The loss of any one of these images, as well as Grace's betrayal of her friendship, would have been substantial. But to suffer all these losses at once simply demolished Eileen's ability to hold on or cope.

Because everything was so bleak wherever she looked, Eileen, unlike the other characters in this chapter, had no need to artificially devalue her life image. It was already in shambles. Thus, in her own mind, she was left with only one dichotomy—the ultimate decision to be or not to be, to hold on or to let go.

Aside from Margaret's death, the multiple losses that befell Eileen came as a result of her sexual orientation: the blackmail and betrayal at the hands of a friend; society's sanctioning of gay and lesbian witch-hunts; the particular homophobia directed to those who work with minors; the vulnerability and fragility of a public reputation; and the continual strain of trying to integrate an ill-fitting hetero-sexual life image. Given factors such as these, it's little wonder that approximately 40 percent of gay men and lesbians have seriously contemplated or attempted sui-cide.[2]

Summary

Chapter 4 dealt with ways in which gays and lesbians keep alive the illusion that they can fit into a heterosexu-ally formed life image. In contrast, this chapter shows how they can react in an opposite fashion separating themselves from the losses by denying the importance of something or someone that was once a cherished element of their being.

This tendency to dichotomize, to split reality into either/or terms, may look pathological, but it's often a nat-ural and helpful part of the process of moving away from that which has been lost. There is a tendency in the hold-ing-on phase to romanticize or idealize that which is in danger of being lost. To counterbalance this, sometimes an extreme reaction is needed in the letting-go phase to achieve a more appropriate and realistic perspective.

Life Image. The life image, by its very nature, deals with attachments, and any loss of that vision involves a realigning of what an individual is attached to. The life images of all the people in this chapter were strongly characterized by needs to be loved and to belong—Seth with regard to his father and family; Connie with another woman; Jean with her friends; Peter with the Church; Larry with his teammates; and Eileen with her lover, her community, and her profession.

Rather than allowing themselves to experience a gradual shift in the nature of their attachments, these six people let go by abruptly severing their relationships with the people and things integral to their life images. Letting go is meant to reduce dependence on attachments, not to destroy them, in order for a reformulated life image to emerge. As can be seen by the cases in this chapter, the process is often more difficult and seemingly destructive for some than for others.

Coping Reactions. Disgust seemed to be one of the coping devices used by all the individuals in this chapter to let go of a shattered life image. Ironically, the disgust was focused on that which had been the very source of their love and nurturance, and served as a means to eradicate it from their systems. Thus, the once potent influence was rejected.

There are actions and feelings that people can substitute for grief over their lost life dreams. Connie used flight as a strategy to separate herself from her pain. Jean and Larry gave in to addictive behaviors, Seth replaced guilt for grief, and quite possibly Eileen's suicide was her way to avoid the massive amount of grieving that lay before her.

Even though some use of letting-go strategies is essential for the eventual transformation of a life image, there is a danger of prolonged reliance on these strategies. If excessive withdrawal, negative focusing, dichotomization, or pessimism are used consistently and over time, they can become a virtually automatic and exclusive way of coping with the pain of loss. In this regard, Connie and Jean may be stuck at the holding-on stage. The jury is still out on Peter, Larry, and Seth.

Lessons. The phase of letting go can serve as a transition or a dead end for individuals who have suffered the trauma of loss. The following lessons may facilitate a more productive passage to the next phase of loss.

1. Thinking in extreme either/or terms can lead you to do things you might later regret.

2. Don't burn bridges; you might want to cross over them some day.

3. When you're feeling negative and cynical, remember that these feelings may be stepping-stones on the path from loss to transformation.

4. Even the most negative emotions are legitimate forms of grieving over a loss, but beware of acting on them.

5. Be careful not to alienate all your friends; you may need them in your old age.

6. Remember during the letting-go stage that the expression of negative emotion may later come back to visit you.

7. Withdrawal that leads to prolonged isolation may become a prelude to dropping out.

6

Awareness of Loss

Most people get fleeting glimpses of the extent of their losses somewhere in the midst of holding-on or letting-go processes. When attempts to manage distress and fear and to keep their life images intact prove unsuccessful, people are defenseless in the face of loss. At this juncture grieving individuals are at the lowest point in the loss process. They realize that what was lost is truly gone, not to be reclaimed or won back ever again. Sadness and grief overwhelm them and the pain is intense. Being totally preoccupied with the past and what was lost, they lack the ability to imagine the future. Their life image, with all their expectations about how the future was to unfold, lies in shambles, and they finally realize that reconstruction is not possible. It is truly a time of crisis in which their belief system and even their will to live is frequently tested.

The cases that illustrate this phase of awareness are necessarily bleak, but they are far from hopeless. After many attempts to ward it off, the full extent of loss finally strikes home for the individuals described. These people have hit an emotional bottom. However, because of the physically and emotionally exhausting nature of this phase, most people don't remain here for long. If they can find the courage to stay with their pain and learn from their loneliness and hopelessness, they place themselves in a favorable position to gain perspective on their loss.

Questioning Life's Meaning

Ellen and George dated in high school and were married while he was in divinity school studying to be a minister. Ellen completely devoted herself to her husband and her responsibilities as a minister's wife, and her life image was totally entwined with her husband's church and "their" ministry. George was most proud of his outreach to homosexuals and of his unrelenting efforts at converting them from their sinful lifestyle and bringing them to repent and stand upright before the Lord. Over the years, Ellen helped with the support groups for "recovering homosexuals" but felt very uncomfortable doing so. She couldn't understand why until she met Lorraine in one of the groups.

From the very beginning, Lorraine proved vocally resistant to the conversion process, so George assigned Ellen the ministry of softening Lorraine's heart to God's word. Spending time together helped Ellen understand her own uneasiness, and the possibility that she herself was lesbian compelled her to seek professional counseling. Within a year, she felt it necessary to leave George, while retaining her membership in the church. During this time, she dated Lorraine and began to fall in love. Soon the congregation heard of her relationship and made it clear that she and Lorraine were no longer members of the community. Her efforts at finding another church proved disappointingly unsuccessful, and eventually she began to recognize that there was no place for a lesbian woman within her denomination. Additionally, the longer she and Lorraine were together the more Ellen realized she was involved with a female counterpart of a rigidly controlling George. In time, their relationship dissolved.

Without a church or partner of her own, Ellen finally was forced to come face to face with the loss of her life image. No longer was she a woman with a place and a purpose. Those beliefs and relationships that had shaped her life had disintegrated. She felt completely empty inside, and sadness was her constant companion. She felt stripped of all that had been meaningful, and the future seemed to hold little possibility for her happiness.

In contrast to previous stages, during the phase of awareness, there appears to be little external movement on the part of the grieving. The mind may be going in a thousand directions at once, while emotionally and perhaps physically there may be a sense of "flattening out" or winding down. Most of the activity is internal, happening close to the center of the person's being. For example, Ellen's life image as a minister's wife provided her with a sense of rightness, respectability, and acceptability. A dawning consciousness of her sexual orientation and its impact on her total belief system set off a frenzied effort to hold on to her crumbling life structure. Neither her attempt to remain within her congregation nor her relationship with the George-like Lorraine served to keep her image of herself intact. Having exhausted her avenues for holding on, Ellen found herself confronted with a crisis of faith. With little to believe in, no roles left in which she could fit, and no guidelines to direct her life, she felt the meaninglessness of her present existence. The full extent of losing the foundations of her life image struck home.

Withdrawing in Silence

Nick's divorce from Sandra was a messy, conflictual affair. She did not want a gay father raising Betsy and Jeff, ages nine and ten, and set about using all legal means possible to discredit Nick. He, in turn, hired expensive attorneys to defend himself against her accusations of moral depravity. Although he lost joint custody, he was granted the right for Betsy and Jeff to visit one night a week. Part of Sandra's strategy in turning the children against Nick was to have them sit in the courtroom and listen to the testimony against Nick's ability to be an effective parent given his gay "lifestyle." This scheme worked: they became so repelled that they refused to see him or even to talk with him on the phone.

Nick saw himself as a father. In spite of the fact that for years he had felt himself caught between his sexuality and his marriage, he had never wavered in his devotion to Betsy and Jeff. When they would no longer have anything to do with him, his world collapsed. Without his children acting as stabilizing forces for his life image, he set about convincing himself that they weren't important to him, anyway. He reasoned to himself that, since no one seemed to give a damn, he might as well behave as Sandra and her lawyers said all homosexuals behave.

Nick thus began to act like a single, childless man on the prowl. As he stashed his children's pictures away in a bottom drawer, he deceived himself into believing that it was a relief to be rid of Betsy and Jeff and their camping trips, ball games, dental appointments, and constant struggles over possession of the channel changer. He joined a gym, changed his hairstyle, and spent many nights in gay bars looking for the perfect lover or at least the perfect one-night stand.

One night, when he was in bed with an attractive man he had had his eye on for some time, the phone rang. A nurse in the hospital emergency room was on the line telling him that his daughter had been brought in with intense abdominal pain and his signature was needed on some insurance forms. He raced to the hospital, signed the papers, and sat in the surgery waiting room while Betsy had her appendix removed. Even though Betsy still acted coldly toward Nick in the days following the operation, the entire experience impressed upon him how much his children meant to him. He knew he was a father and not just a childless single man, but there was no way to live out that image without Jeff and Betsy's participation. His awareness of this seemingly impossible bind sent him into a deep depression. He no longer had the energy to go to bars or to seek out sexual companions. Outside of work, all of his time was spent in his apartment crying and grieving over what he had lost. The images of his children and himself as a father constantly floated to the surface of his mind. His efforts at letting go had failed, and he could no longer pretend that his children were unimportant to him. He was weak and exhausted and needed time in solitude to heal.

Unlike Ellen, who delayed her awareness by holding on to a nonviable life image, Nick engaged in letting-go behaviors to remove from his consciousness the loss of his children and his parental role. Awareness of the extent of loss, the breaking through denial to the unglossed reality, marks a turning point in the grieving process. Efforts at minimizing loss are no longer effective, and often even a seemingly minor event can break the pattern. In Nick's case, Betsy's surgery served to cut through his self-deception and make him confront the magnitude of his grief over the loss of his children.

With the buffers removed and the full impact of the loss having become conscious, Nick mourned by withdrawing from behaviors he had adopted to diminish his grief. This pulling back, in many ways, felt to him like the awareness he initially had after losing his children in the divorce, but it was even more painful this time. The now-undeniable dismantling of his life image left him feeling alone, hopeless, and helpless.

Deciding to Live

Fran and Bill had been married for thirty years. Their only child, Clark, called them on his twenty-fifth birthday, said he wasn't feeling well, and asked if he could come home to live with them. They had known for some time that Clark was gay, and their fears about the cause of his illness were soon confirmed. Clark's AIDS progressed rapidly, and Fran, who worked at home, devoted herself to caring for him.

Clark's last months of life brought the family closer together, and when Clark died, Fran, being the primary caregiver, was especially distraught. She couldn't seem to come to terms with her loss. Her mourning and despair

116

were so intense that one night she gathered Clark's left-over sleeping pills and swallowed them all. Bill discovered her unconscious body and rushed her to the hospital, where her life was saved.

When Fran returned home from the hospital, she looked to Bill for support and strength. She had always considered him to be the stronger one and was shocked to find him withdrawn and often on the brink of crying. When she found out he had quit his garden club and no longer joined "the boys" for an after-work beer, she knew that one of them had to make a decision to live through this. Before Clark's death, her family life image had consisted of three people. She now fully realized that she had lost one of these people, but she was not about to lose another. She told Bill that they had lost a child but that they hadn't lost each other; together they had to find the strength to live through this experience.

When the extent of the loss is realized, the will to live is often challenged. In other words, when Fran's life image and all that seemed meaningful for her was severely threatened, she nearly gave up on life. It was only when the reality of Bill's deterioration hit home that she clearly chose to continue living. Bill's withdrawal from the garden club and his friends became for her moments of truth containing the same symbolic impact as the moments when Nick signed the insurance forms and Ellen saw the George-like qualities in Lorraine.

It is at these times of demise of their illusions and awareness of the nonviability of their life dreams that individuals are at a true point of choice. In order to move on with life, they have to relinquish their attempts to buffer pain, let the full awareness of what they have lost become a reality, and in many cases make a conscious decision to live.

Confronting Helplessness

Ever since coming out as a gay man, Taylor had entertained a life image of being an attorney who championed the civil rights of gay men and lesbians. After law school, he took a job in the county prosecutor's office. A case came before them in which two brothers allegedly murdered a gay man in a rural section of the county. The case centered upon the defendants' contentions that the gay man had approached them for sex and that they had become so frightened that they had shot the "fag" three times through the head. The entire case, especially the "homosexual panic" defense, interested Taylor, and his supervisor consented to his serving as prosecutor.

Taylor won the case, and the two brothers were sent to prison. Once the sentencing was complete, some male relatives of the defendants decided to pass their own sentence on this "queer lawyer" who had made fools of their family members. One day after work, several of them trapped him in the parking garage and would have beaten him to death had a security guard not sounded an alarm. Taylor was terrified for his life and so badly battered that it took him months to recover physically. During this period of extended recuperation at home, he played out many mental scenarios, the most recurrent being that of prosecuting the men who beat him up and others like them who prey on lesbian and gay people. The full reality of his situation didn't penetrate his consciousness until the case against the thugs who hurt him was summarily dismissed on a technicality.

The dismissal completely undermined his life image as the champion of gay civil rights. How could he possibly stand up for the rights of others when he couldn't even serve as his own friend in court? The shattering of his illusions about his own competence and the ability of the justice system to defend gay men and lesbians left him feeling powerless and helpless. With his confidence in himself and his belief in the legal structure at such a low ebb, he could envision no viable or productive future for himself in the practice of law.

Taylor's case illustrates the shattering of his life image and the destruction of assumptions that underlie it. Like many lesbian and gay victims of assault, Taylor's beliefs about fairness, safety, and belonging were violated. When he was attacked, his illusion that justice could prevail for individuals of same-gender orientation and that he could be an instrument of that justice crumbled.

Taylor's case also places into clear perspective the key elements of hopelessness and helplessness. The awareness of the extent of loss implies a running out of options: it becomes impossible to ward off further the full impact of the loss. All the individuals discussed so far in this chapter felt these emotions and encountered the realities of a future seemingly devoid of hope and a present marked by the apparent collapse of their ability to cope. Taylor's beating left him angry and combative, holding on to his life image as the champion of due process ready to do battle with gay-bashing enemies. It was only when his own case failed to go forward to trial that his complete helplessness and impotence at effecting justice was exposed for all, especially those who had placed their hopes in him, to see.

Encountering Memories

Colette, an elementary school teacher, had not seen her mother for many years. At their last meeting, Colette had told her widowed mother, Florence, that she was lesbian and was in love with another woman. Florence, who was usually the soul of calmness, reacted with uncharacteristic fear, anger, and harshness. She couldn't get beyond the word "lesbian," and it was as if it conjured the emergence of another being from within her. She began repeating, "I'm so ashamed, I'm so ashamed, I'm so ashamed." She also said, "I won't have such filth in my home and I don't want to hear that word ever again." She told Colette that until she could get those thoughts out of her mind, she was not to come home. Colette was in a state of shock and silently left her mother's home. Her feelings eventually turned to anger, which made her resolve never to return.

On an impulse, fifteen years later, Colette decided to call Florence on Mother's Day. Her physically disabled sister Elinor, who had always lived at home, answered the phone and almost apologetically told Colette that Mom had died two months ago. Elinor explained that Florence didn't want Colette to be contacted in the event of her death. On first hearing the news, Colette was numb, but then she became furious. She once again felt deeply violated by her mother. She never had understood why Mom had seemed to take her lesbianism so personally. She decided that her best course of action was to put her mother far from her consciousness and get on with her life. After all, she had lived without her for fifteen years and she could certainly continue to do so now. Mom had forgotten her, and she would do the same.

Some time later, Colette was standing in front of the bathroom mirror and was stunned by the realization of how much she had come to resemble Mom. At this point, all efforts to remove her mother from her life dissipated. She stood frozen before the mirror for a long time as maternal memories broke through her consciousness. It seemed that so many things about herself from that day onward reminded her of Mom—the way she disciplined the children at school, her tone of voice, the way she wrung her hands when she grew frustrated. These ever-present reminders impressed upon Colette how deeply her mother was still a part of her and how much she really missed her. These feelings compelled Colette to return to her mother's home and once again be among Florence's things. She wanted to walk where Mom had walked and touch the things that Mom had touched. Elinor gave her some old boxes of family pictures and mementos to look through. There, at the bottom of a box in a yellowed envelope, Colette found two letters written to Florence forty years before from Ruth, her childhood chum. In the letters, Ruth described how much she loved Florence and how she only wished that circumstances were different and they could enjoy each other's embraces forever. The knowledge of her mother's secret, and its accompanying sadness and shame, intensified Colette's own deep sadness, and she sat on the closet floor and wept.

One of the reasons this phase of loss was so painful for Colette was that the memories that came to flood her mind were so deeply rooted in her family life image. For so long, she had been disconnected from an image of herself as a member of her family of origin, especially as a loving daughter and accepted child. The memories that now occupied her consciousness were bittersweet in that they both reconnected her with her family and mother and reminded her that she was an orphan. With Florence dead, symbolically there was no going home again, no way to revive a life image that had passed with her mother. The full awareness of this brought Colette intense emptiness and heartbreak. Her anguish was only compounded by the revelation of her mother's secret torment. Unlike the overly negative memories involved in letting go or the bigger-than-life remembrances of holding on, the memories Colette encountered were unglossed and unable to buffer her pain.

Imaging an Empty Future

Juanita and Rose had been together for ten years and desperately wanted a child. Juanita, who came from a large Hispanic family, always had imagined herself as a mother, nurturing children of her own. They repeatedly had tried to adopt a child but ran into continual roadblocks with the county or state welfare department. They were even turned down when they applied to parent a foster child. In the face of such consistent denials, Juanita suspected a bias existed against their lesbian couplehood, even though nothing was ever said directly to either of them.

There was a lot of talk in the lesbian community about women being impregnated with frozen sperm, and several of their friends had given birth. Juanita and Rose decided that they also wanted to try artificial insemination and were willing to devote their savings to the costly and possible futile procedures. Because Rose had recently had a hysterectomy, Juanita would be the birth mother.

Month after month, Juanita tried to get pregnant. She repeatedly got her hopes up, only to be disillusioned. Finally, the physician at the clinic told her that any further inseminations would prove fruitless. Juanita can still remember the look on the doctor's face as she told her that her chances of becoming pregnant were virtually nonexistent. At that moment, Juanita realized that her image of herself as a mother was no longer achievable. She had exhausted all avenues for making her dream come true, and now she was confronted with the awful truth.

Juanita had so focused her vision of the future on a child that life without a baby seemed bleak. She could not imagine herself and Rose attending family gatherings with all the nieces and nephews reminding them of their child-lessness. A future without an infant to rock, children's birthday parties, lunches to pack, and a small mouth to feed was hardly imaginable. Juanita found herself obsessed with thinking about the baby she didn't have, and the world was telescoped through her loss. She was preoccupied with babies, and reminders were everywhere.

Juanita had made every effort to avoid the possible reality of a future without offspring of her own. When all her attempts failed, the full awareness of her dismantled life image hit home. As so often happens when the extent of reality becomes apparent, Juanita became so preoccupied with the object of her loss that she couldn't envision a future without a baby.

In this awareness phase, everything from chance conversations to the sights, sounds, and smells of everyday life can bring with them thoughts about the loss. Nothing is sacred, and everything seems to relate back to the loss—the loss for Juanita was her baby, for Nick his children, for Fran and Bill their son Clark, and for Colette her mother. All of these people were so preoccupied with past losses and the implications of these for the present that their ability to imagine the future with any sense of hope seemed impossible.

Summary

The phase of awareness of loss is characterized by a face-to-face encounter with the reality and extent of shattered life images. In many ways, it is the low point of the loss process in that it signals the futility of efforts to reduce or minimize loss by using either holding-on or letting-go strategies.

At this point in the loss process, most people find themselves immersed in thoughts of what was lost, assailed by memories of what had been, and possibly obsessed with their present loss and grief. The future is hardly imaginable, containing little possibility for hope or happiness. Frequently, all that had seemed sacred is doubted, and what was once held meaningful, even the person's own life, is called into question. Emotions are intense during this time, and feelings of sadness, hopelessness, and helplessness are common. People often withdraw into their sorrow and experience periods of heavy sighing and weeping.

Life Image. With the exception of Taylor, the losses of the people described in this chapter began with a dismantling of their familial life images. Their assumptions about how they expected to act out their roles within a family context simply were not going to be realized. For Ellen, it was her role as minister's wife that was central to her life image, for Nick it was Betsy and Jeff, for Fran and Bill it was Clark, for Colette it was her mother, and for Juanita it was a baby. The context of Taylor's loss was his life work and his image of himself as a champion of justice for gay men and lesbians. In every case, the unavoidable awareness that their life images had shattered brought these people to a point of crisis.

Coping Reactions. The people in this chapter exemplify behaviors typical of the awareness phase. All of them were emerging from a process of holding on/letting go and were left exhausted, with few defenses to continue the battle against confronting the reality of loss. They seemed to be in a world of their own, lost in their pain, flooded with memories, and thus isolated emotionally from others. Unlike the reactive, escapelike distancing of the letting-go phase, the aloneness of the individuals experiencing an awareness of the extent of their loss had less of a toxic quality—they were not as much fleeing from bitter reality as defenselessly waiting for potential healing.

In addition to these common qualities, the six characters had their own personal reactions to the passage into awareness. Ellen anguished over the meaninglessness of her life, Nick withdrew into aloneness, and Fran and Bill made the crucial decision to live. In contrast to Nick's pulling back voluntarily, Taylor's convalescence provided an involuntary withdrawal from life, possibly exacerbating the contemplation of his hopelessness and helplessness. Awareness brought Colette a flood of bittersweet memories and brought Juanita a preoccupation and obsession over the baby she would never have.

Lessons. The awareness phase can be extremely painful, even though the intensity of emotion usually rises and falls over time. The lessons below are designed to help maximize the benefits of this stage.

1. Have the courage to stay with your sadness; remember that your feelings, though they may be painful, can lead to transformation.

2. Be patient with yourself when grieving, and keep yourself safe and comfortable.

3. The awareness phase is a time of waiting and not the time to accomplish great feats.

4. Beware of over-reliance on mind-altering substances, lest by depriving yourself of pain, you also deprive yourself of its lessons.

5. Don't despair; awareness feels like initial shock, but it is a prelude to perspective.

6. Remember, when in pain, that you have to see something for what it is in order eventually to gain perspective.

7. Find those people who can tell you the truth even though it might sting, but don't ask before you are ready to hear it.

7

Gaining Perspective

The phases of loss are more cyclical than linear and more entwined than separate or discrete. Times of awareness are interspersed with efforts to hold on and let go, until the individual becomes cognizant of the full extent of the loss and experiences the pain and helplessness that accompany awareness. In this chapter, yet another phase begins to interplay with those already described. In this stage of gaining perspective, people seem to turn a corner on their sadness, feel less preoccupied by their loss, and are more ready to make peace with the past. In a sense, the scars left by their mutilated life images are quietly, almost imperceptibly being healed.

The six individuals introduced in this chapter made a choice somewhere within the intense pain of the awareness phase of their losses. Rather than retreating back to exercises that would limit consciousness of their anguish, they opened themselves to seeing the loss from new perspectives and fresh points of view. They can thus be seen balancing the scales of their lives and beginning to assimilate the positive with what had previously seemed entirely negative.

Healing Memories

Helen and Myra had been partners for forty-one years.
They had met during World War II when they both
worked in a textile factory in Vermont. Before most people even knew what the term *lesbian* meant, Helen and
Myra fell in love. They formed a committed relationship
and supported each other during the deaths of four parents. Over the years, they came to be seen by younger
women as a model for long-term lesbian couples.

Myra was first diagnosed with breast cancer a few
days after the gala celebration of their fortieth anniver-
sary. A year later, she was dead. Helen grieved deeply,
alternating between enshrining Myra's memory and being
angry at her for dying. When the full awareness of her
loss set in, Helen was so preoccupied with her sadness
that she needed to take a leave of absence from her job.
Spending time at home helped her place the loss of Myra
into perspective. She surrounded herself with their
favorite music and spent time looking through their old
photo albums and slides. Helen had done this many
times before, but this time was different. The solitude
helped create an inner atmosphere of peace and softness,
and she was able to begin separating herself from the
pain of her loss. Helen reminisced about her times with
Myra and found herself overwhelmed with gratitude for
their forty-one years of marriage. She chuckled about
their parties and private moments together and felt the
acrid tears that came from knowing that these no longer
existed. Helen's pain eventually became less intense, her
sense of struggle diminished, and the process of healing
began.

Like the awareness stage, the period of gaining perspective is an interior experience, with most changes occurring in the emotions. Once Helen took time away from her work, these "changes of the heart" happened in the solitude of her home and in the sanctuary of her memories. Her life image was centered on a committed, loving relationship with another woman. As would any widow, she deeply mourned that the person so integral to that image was gone. After much struggling, this period of peace enabled Helen to convalesce and heal.

Balancing Perceptions

Tim experienced feelings of intense betrayal when he learned that his lover of five years, Patrick, had been consistently unfaithful during most of their relationship. He felt even more duped when he discovered that several of their close mutual friends had known of the deception and hadn't told him. Tim's sense of humiliation drove him to leave Patrick and write off their friends as coconspirators. He was so embarrassed and hurt that he moved out of town so he would never have to face any of them again.

A year later, around Christmas time, Tim came back for a visit with his family. One evening he went down to the town's only gay bar to see who was still around. The first person he saw was Patrick with his new lover and several of the "coconspirators." This scene sent Tim into a frenzy. He fled the bar, got into his car, and accelerated out of town onto a country road. Being too preoccupied to see the warning signs, he missed the curve, flipped his car, and rolled down a ravine.

Tim was hospitalized for many months, and his recuperation was an arduous process both physically and mentally. During this time, he realized how much he missed Patrick and his friends and the good times they had all enjoyed together. Tim's grief over the loss of his friendship network could no longer be denied. His emotional pain lessened, and his outlook on Patrick and his old friends began to shift so that he was able to see them in a clearer perspective. He acknowledged that he had occasionally enjoyed a trick or two behind Patrick's back. And what he had regarded as a conspiracy of silence on his friends' part was probably their way of protecting him from extremely bad news. Tim became aware, too, that no one was to blame for the loss. This balancing of perceptions helped to soften his feelings to the point that he could imagine himself walking into the bar, seeing Patrick with his new lover and friends, and being detached enough to remain calm, forgiving, and accepting of his loss.

Both Helen and Tim lost the sources of nurturance and belonging intrinsic to their life images. In Tim's vision of himself he was part of a lifetime network of friends, with Patrick at his side. Had the tragedy of his car accident not occurred and had he continued to denigrate his relationships by feeding on resentment, he might never have gained the perspective necessary to move beyond his bitterness. His period of recovery granted him the solitude he needed to balance his perceptions and regain his equilibrium.

Rediscovering Life

Amelia had rarely left her house since the bar she once owned and operated folded last year. She bought the bar fifteen years before with the vision of providing a place where gay men and lesbians could freely socialize. The Lotus Inn soon became a hub, with Amelia at the center, serving as a combination of welcoming hostess, listening heart, and boisterous cheerleader who set the tone for nightly merriment.

To this day, Amelia has trouble understanding what went wrong and why people stopped coming. She knew the AIDS crisis had prompted many to stop drinking, and even the women appeared to get in on the act. It seemed they just dropped her and began meeting in "those damned support groups for this and that." Whatever the case, she found she could not pay her monthly bills and one day had to shut the doors of the Lotus Inn for the last time.

With the money she had saved over the years, she took a year off to sort things out. She alternated between raging at the ingratitude of her ex-patrons and missing them deeply. She was furious at them for taking their loyalties elsewhere and at the same time felt deprived of her role as proprietor par excellence of the most popular gay bar in town.

One day, Mildred, the elderly lady next door, asked Amelia to help her build a fence around the flower garden in order to keep the neighbor's German shepherd from running through it. Amelia knew that Mildred had lost her two sons during World War II and that her husband of sixty-three years had recently died. He and Mildred had tended the garden during most of his retirement years, and they had often sat together under an arbor holding hands at the end of the day.

Amelia was happy to dig postholes and carry the fence posts for Mildred as well as listen to the stories of this eighty-five-year-old woman. This prompted something to shift in Amelia, and she found herself reminiscing about her days at the Lotus Inn. As she told her stories, she began to assimilate some of Mildred's attitude of acceptance in the face of tragedy and her ability to find peace in tending her garden. During Amelia's days working alongside Mildred, she felt her anger drain away, and, for the first time that year, she heard the birds singing.

To gain perspective, there must come a time when feelings of anger and struggle begin to ebb and waves of forgiveness and acceptance quietly start to take their place. In Amelia's case, she was able to rediscover life by listening to Mildred talk about the perspective she gained after she lost her sons and husband. In some ways, Amelia's and Mildred's life images were similar in that both women saw themselves as occupying a central position within a group of special people and providing them with love and nurturance. Amelia learned by working next to Mildred that life doesn't end with shattered dreams but can be appreciated anew by listening to the wisdom of age and quietly tending nature's garden.

Admitting Responsibility

Mitch described his home life as "murderous and miserable." His stepfather would drink until he became abusive and take out his anger on Mitch while Mitch's mother would cry helplessly and be totally ineffectual in her attempts to protect her son. Mitch seemed to remember the situation getting worse as he grew older until finally, at age seventeen, he packed his few belongings, took a commuter train, and headed for the big city. He was fortunate to find work as an errand boy for a large department store, and this enabled him to get a small room in which to live.

Loneliness compelled him to look for other gay men like himself. Although he had little money, his good looks and natural charm gave him an open invitation to join a fast-living crowd where alcohol and drugs were readily available and partying was nonstop on weekends. He felt exhilarated by the acceptance he was experiencing and thought that he had arrived at last. His newfound friends were at first willing to underwrite his escalating use of drugs, but eventually they insisted that he come up with his own money. This made him work harder at the store, and he was soon promoted from errand boy to sales clerk to department manager. He continued to live in his rented room and spent the money he saved on his increasingly expensive drug habit. Over time, he resorted to petty theft at work and to mooching off his dwindling number of friends. He even stole money from coats and wallets at parties and from his mother's purse on his infrequent visits home.

Mitch eventually was fired for stealing from the company. Because he could no longer pay the rent, he was forced to give up his room. Three weeks of living on the streets was enough to convince him that he needed help. One day, he walked into a gay and lesbian recovery house and confessed that he was a drug addict and that he wanted to come clean. During his early recovery, he blamed everyone but himself—his stepfather who beat him up, his mother who didn't protect him, his friends who led him astray by hooking him on drugs to support

135

their own habits, and his bosses who fired him without hearing his side of the story. During his six-week stay at the recovery house, Mitch realized that he was powerless over drugs, committed himself to a program of sobriety, and obtained a job for which his counselor had recommended him. It was only after a year of faithfully following a twelve-step program that he was able to admit responsibility for his addiction, acknowledge his wrongdoing toward others, and forgive himself for his imperfection and human frailty. With these new perspectives, he was better able to cooperate with his healing and recovery.

One of the core tasks involved in gaining perspective is acknowledging the extent and limits of one's own and others' responsibility for the loss. In trying to realize his life image of belonging and mattering to people with whom he bonded, Mitch surrendered his perspective to the power of drugs. By playing the role of the fair-haired newcomer, he was able to overcome some of the rejection of his childhood, but he quickly set himself up once again to be a victim. Time and perspective eventually allowed him to balance his tendency to blame his persecutors with acceptance of his own responsibility for assuming a bogus life image and bringing about his own loss.

Taking Time

When Donna completed her training program as a registered nurse, she returned to her hometown with her lover, Blanca, to care for her widowed father. Because of her skill and hard work, she quickly rose to the position of nursing supervisor. Dad lived with Donna and Blanca and enjoyed the small circle of their lesbian friends who came over every Friday night to fix dinner and play cards. Because it was such a small town, the group rarely socialized outside the home for fear of harassment or job discrimination.

However, rumors began to spread at the hospital about unmarried Donna and Blanca, her constant companion. Donna was a strikingly beautiful woman; it was not uncommon for men to ask her for a date, for which she would thank them but politely refuse. One day, she walked into the coffee room and overheard one man tell another, "What a ball busting dyke." Gradually, she came to notice small incidents such as coworkers stopping in mid-conversation when she entered the nurses' lounge, subordinates "forgetting" to do tasks she had assigned, and administrators glancing at her with bemused looks even when she was explaining something quite serious.

All of this began to play in Donna's thoughts and caused her a great deal of inner turmoil and pain. Swimming through her mind were questions such as "Who knows what? What are people saying? What does that look mean?" She felt that her reputation and position were being undermined. In an effort to regain her status, she worked doubly hard at her job and took care never to go out in public with Blanca. When the rumors persisted, she became angry, but she was coming to realize that her pretense of heterosexuality was no longer tenable.

One day, Dad said, "They may not love or respect you because you are lesbian, but I do. You may not have the worth in their eyes that you do in mine. I am proud to be in your and Blanca's home." His words penetrated Donna's anger and enabled her to begin gaining some perspective on her sorrow. She knew she had lost something, but the loss seemed so nebulous that she was unable to define precisely what it was. In order to get a handle on it, she sensed she needed to take time, be willing to live with the vulnerability that comes with ambiguity, and be patient with herself and not rush toward some facile but premature resolution of the situation.

Donna's experience demonstrates that loss can sometimes be nebulous and undefinable while still being painful and debilitating. She knew that something essential to her life image of competence and respectability was being undermined and she took holding-on and letting-go steps to help salvage that loss. Her father's words brought home the reality of her lost reputation and succeeded in planting the seeds for the rebirth of a more viable life image. And unlike the four individuals so far seen in this chapter, Donna gained perspective on her loss not by a period of solitude and withdrawal, but by the equally effective means of being patient with her vulnerability while continuing on with life.

Getting Set Back

Brad thought he was finally experiencing a sense of peace and acceptability about being gay when the antidiscrimination ordinance came up for a vote in his city. The growth in perspective and personal balance that he had struggled so hard to gain was thoroughly undermined as news reports indicated that large numbers of

138

individuals within his own community vehemently reviled gay men and lesbians. In their expressions of hatred and shame, he could hear his own voice not so long ago condemning himself for being gay. Just as he was beginning to quell his own homophobia, he saw how extensive and caustic it was around him. Hearing statements like "homosexuals deserve condemnation by those who uphold traditional morality" and "such a filthy lifestyle warrants the law's severest judgment rather than its protection" set Brad back to the point where again he wished he weren't gay.

When the city ordinance experience occurred, Brad was beginning to develop a softened and harmonious perspective about his sexuality and had even begun to contemplate the possibility of establishing a permanent relationship. His initial awareness of his sexual orientation had come in high school as a result of an encounter with a classmate. This terrified him and left him with a profound sense of self-loathing and shame. He spent many years trying to pretend he was heterosexual, but deep down he knew that when he watched X-rated movies, he paid more attention to the man than the woman, and when he viewed big-time wrestling on TV, he had more interest in the bodies than in the sport. When he could no longer maintain his denial, reality broke through and thrust him into a deep depression. What had seemed most repugnant to him was inescapably a part of his nature. Brad knew he was gay and he hated himself for it.

Knowing that he could no longer contain his secret, he turned in desperation to a college professor in the community who was known for his advocacy of gay issues and his willingness to help lesbian and gay people in distress. Dr. Norm proved to be an angel in disguise. With his help, Brad came to see new dimensions to his loss and grew to a sense of balance and healing about his sexual orientation. His self-esteem rose, and he started to see some of the virtues of being different from the rest of the population. It was at this point that the fallout from the ordinance brought back to consciousness the full force of Brad's initial revulsion.

Brad's earliest life image, like everyone's, was one of heterosexuality and integration with the dominant culture. When this shattered, he descended into depression, but eventually he gained perspective through the good mentoring of Dr. Norm. As a result, he began to formulate a revised life image, one in which gay people like himself were accepted and respected members of society. The acrimonious and condemnatory reactions of his fellow citizens to the antidiscrimination ordinance undermined the viability of his newly emerging vision of his place in society.

This kind of setback is not uncommon in journeying through loss. Recovery from loss, in fact, is rarely sequential but often involves what may appear to be regressions to previous stages. In Brad's case, the setback to earlier homophobia occurred just when he was beginning to gain perspective on his sexuality and his self-worth. Just as he was confronted with a choice point before he went to Dr. Norm, so again the new awareness of reality placed him at another such juncture—to shut down or to continue the arduous task of refining yet again his life image.

Summary

Persons in the gaining-perspective phase are beginning to feel a sense of healing and a certain peace with the past. The emotional intensity connected with the loss has lessened. Often, the balm of time and solitude succeeds in softening the pain, although it is rarely eliminated forever. Even though setbacks can and do occur, individuals are often turning the corner on their grief with the onset of this phase. What had once been experienced as thoroughly negative can now be seen to have positive, even life-giving elements. The emotional energy that was invested in the past is freed to be channeled elsewhere.

Life Image. Belonging is usually a central theme in the life images of gay men and lesbians, the majority of whom have felt like outsiders most of their lives. Crucial to understanding the individuals in this chapter is their need to have a sense of place and to matter to some significant person(s).

Helen saw herself and Myra growing old together. Tim viewed himself by Patrick's side and in the company of lifelong friends. While Amelia's life image had her assuming center stage in the process of nurturing people and gathering them together, Mitch wanted to position himself in life's fast lane. Both of them, however, needed to belong and to matter. Donna sought to matter on the professional level—being respected and seen as competent. Brad initially envisioned himself as an accepted heterosexual citizen; failing this, he pictured himself as an esteemed gay member of society. These six life images became dismembered, and the individuals had to struggle to gain perspective on the finality of their loss.

Reactions. A major reaction at this phase is the overall reduction of emotional intensity, characterized by patience and the tendency to release more readily hostility, anger, and resentments. Amelia came to feel less angry at her patrons; Tim at Patrick and his "coconspirators"; Helen at Myra for leaving; Mitch at his parents, friends, and boss; Donna at her coworkers; and Brad at his homophobic self and society. Accompanying this softening of feeling comes a diminished need to struggle at reversing the loss or to continue doing battle with fate.

As perceptions become more balanced, people often are more willing to forgive and accept themselves, others, or the incomprehensible powers that seem to direct their lives. Even losses that seem nebulous can be accepted with increased serenity. When setbacks occur, balance, peace, and perspective have a greater chance of being regained.

Lessons. The time of gaining perspective is a time of taking it easy and balancing the negative and positive aspects of the loss. The lessons below are offered to help in healing and making peace with the past.

1. Life can be rediscovered by being open to and receiving the lessons of nature—but you may have to sit quietly and listen.

2. The experiences and stories of those who have passed through tragedy can often inspire you to assume new perspectives.

3. Don't cling too tightly to your newfound insights, because as time goes on, perspectives usually shift.

4. Be patient and beware of forcing perspectives, because pressures to resolve losses too hastily might end up prolonging the process.

5. If you find yourself set back to the beginning of the loss process, don't blow it out of proportion. Remember, you've been here before and can do it again.

6. Keep in mind that losses are intertwined, and if several come all at once, gaining perspective on one can give you insight on the others.

7. Formal recovery programs are generally helpful, because the exchange of strengths, hopes, and experiences beats trying to gain perspective alone.

8

Integrating Loss[1]

If people remain at the gaining-perspective phase, they may limit their opportunities to grow from loss. Having attained a certain movement of heart and mind, they are sometimes reluctant to extend themselves in a way that might occasion further loss and pain. They have released any hope of regaining what they had invested in a past life image and are often content to idle in the present with little energy or inclination to envision a future. Other individuals, however, feel an incompleteness or a tension and experience a willingness to cooperate with powers beyond themselves to renew their sense of hope. Their desire for a new life image and for the ability to dream anew prompts them to take the public step necessary to turn themselves toward the future.

The people we will meet in this chapter are attempting actively to integrate their loss. The decision to move on compels them to take a public step that, in some symbolic manner, helps shift the nature of their grief. As they proactively step out of themselves and assume responsibility for their lives, they become even more free of the past and what was lost. Energy that was locked in grief can now be released and reinvested elsewhere. With tensions loosened, the result is often a renewed sense of hope and vision for the future.

Going Public

Jill and Abby had been together twelve years and considered themselves lesbian life partners. At the beginning of their relationship, Abby had invited Jill to move into her condominium and share the mortgage payments with her. Being relatively young and in good health, neither had felt the need to set up a durable power of attorney that would have entrusted legal or medical decisions to the other. Thus, when Abby had a skiing accident, it was possible for her parents to deny Jill hospital visitation rights, since she was not considered part of Abby's immediate family. Abby's parents had never liked Jill and accused her of making their daughter lesbian. They took the occasion of Abby's hospitalization to demonstrate their dislike for Jill by leaving strict instructions at the nursing desk that under no circumstances was Jill to be admitted to the intensive care unit. Their exclusion of Jill from Abby's life continued even after Abby's death. Jill requested that her lover's funeral be held in the city where their friends could attend. But the parents insisted that they were Abby's family and that this was a family decision. Thus, the funeral and burial were conducted in rural Arkansas, two thousand miles away from anyone who knew who Abby really was. Jill attended the funeral alone and was deeply pained by a service that she knew would have offended her lover's spiritual sensibilities.

Several months later, Jill was beginning to gain some perspective on her loss when a court order initiated by

Abby's parents sought her eviction from the condo. Abby's mother and father were the legal beneficiaries of their daughter's estate, because when Jill had moved in and begun splitting mortgage payments with Abby, they had neglected to either draw up a will or put the condo in both names. Thus, with Abby's death, Jill not only lost her partner but her home as well.

Part of Jill didn't want to fight the eviction, but another part knew that she could not come to terms with her many losses without standing up for her integrity and that of Abby. She needed to go public with the problem, so she sought the assistance of a national organization that defended the legal rights of gay men and lesbians. By seeking redress for her grievances, Jill knew that she would be publicly exposed as lesbian. She talked with her parents and boss before allowing the organization to begin the uphill battle to have gay and lesbian domestic partners recognized as similar to heterosexual spouses in all legal matters. She knew that she could immediately end the situation by getting out of the condo and out of the lives of Abby's parents, but this would not satisfy her sense of justice. Her integrity demanded a public step on her own behalf.

Just as perspective begins to diminish grief, integration of loss can occur only after some public step. This step may not be as dramatic as Jill's lawsuit; it may be as understated as writing a letter after many years or as ritualized as placing a flower on a grave. Even though her image of a long life with Abby was no longer obtainable, Jill was able to honor her commitment to their relationship by choosing to have her rights adjudicated publicly in a court of law. She knew that her chances of winning equal rights were slim, but she was willing to step forward and begin a process that others behind her would someday complete. Thus, by not compromising her integrity or foreclosing her conscience or feelings, she was able to consolidate her loss in an appropriate and more satisfying manner.

Finishing Business

Harold's grandfather, Joseph, started his career with the railroad as a porter. His hard work and intelligence eventually ensured his rise first to conductor and then to a position as the first black executive in the company. Joseph's retirement was the occasion for a large family gathering, with relatives coming from near and far to honor the grandson of slaves who had become a prominent railroad executive. Toward the end of the evening, he proudly toasted his three children and eight grandchildren. Harold was the last to be so honored. Instead of the usual words of validation and affection that the other grandchildren received, Harold was subjected to words of shame and rejection. His grandfather publicly hinted at Harold's homosexuality by toasting: "And here's to my grandson Harold, who likes men more than women and from whom I'll never see a great-grandbaby. May he bring no further shame to this family."

It was seven years before Harold could bring himself to face Joseph again. In the meantime, Harold moved into another neighborhood and deliberately avoided every family gathering where his grandfather might be present. During these years, Joseph would occasionally inquire about Harold, and to those who knew him, it was clear that he regretted what he had said about Harold on the night of his retirement.

Harold's initial mortification and intense anger eventually began to dissipate, and, in time, he gained perspective on his damaged reputation within the family and on the loss of respect from his grandfather. One evening when he knew Joseph was at his weekly lodge meeting, he stopped by to see his grandmother, who on several occasions had sent him notes of love and encouragement. She invited Harold to attend a family celebration of her seventy-fifth birthday. He intuitively knew that this was his opportunity to forgive his grandfather publicly and to finish the business that had been festering for too many years.

Harold, like Jill, needed to take a public step in order to address his loss. Harold's image of being a validated and respected grandchild and family member was shattered by his grandfather's remarks. Only a sincere and public act of forgiveness, coming after he had gained appropriate perspective, could complete the cycle of grief and consolidate his identity and pride as a gay man. Harold had to remind himself that the public forgiveness of his grandfather was an act of personal growth. Whether or not Joseph responded positively to this step of integration did not in any way detract from his efforts at moving through his loss.

Emerging From Secrecy

Jack and Mary, a longtime married heterosexual couple, had always wanted a "normal" family, complete with

149

sons- and daughters-in-law and grandchildren. Mary's life dream was composed of images of having an adult daughter as a part of her life and of sharing stories of spouses, child-rearing, cooking, and family history. The only problem with this scenario was that their only daughter, Emma, was lesbian. Emma had told her parents of her orientation when she was still in high school. Jack and Mary had responded caringly but cautioned Emma not to "flaunt" her sexuality in their home town or to mention it to any other family member. They explained that this was a secret "best kept among ourselves," and that if Emma chose to "act out with other women," she would need to do so out of town.

Jack and Mary were particularly uncomfortable at family gatherings when their own brothers and sisters would exchange stories of children and grandchildren. They found themselves avoiding any discussion of Emma's personal life and preferred to focus their conversation on her work. However, Jack and Mary had over the years continued to keep the door of their home open to Emma and her "women friends." They had met quite a few and had come to like them a great deal. Their grief at having a lesbian daughter began to change into a more appreciative and favorable perspective as they saw how happy Emma was with her friends. They listened attentively as the women talked about their own parents, some of whom had joined a parent support organization known as Parents and Friends of Lesbians and Gays.[2]

Gradually, Jack and Mary became uncomfortable with lying to their brothers and sisters about Emma's orientation. Their own sense of shame had diminished and they had become very proud of Emma. They decided to handle differently the inquiries at the next family gathering, which was to be Easter dinner. When the day came and Mary's brother Sherman walked up and asked about Emma's marital possibilities, they both looked him in the eye and said almost in unison, "She's not looking for a husband. She's lesbian."

Jack and Mary's willingness to talk freely of Emma's lesbianism was a far cry from their initial response of secrecy and shame. Their public step was an acknowledgement that a transition had taken place to a new form of relating with Emma. It also symbolized a relinquishing of a life image of a heterosexually married daughter with children. This quiet expression of honesty loosened the tensions they had been carrying for years, allowed them to feel a sense of freedom, and opened them to the possibility of a new life image for themselves and their daughter.

Assuming Responsibility

Gordon accompanied Charles, a childhood friend, to the AIDS testing center to determine if Charlie had been exposed to the AIDS virus. In a show of support, Gordon underwent the test himself. He was shocked when both their tests came back positive. After several more confirming tests, he could no longer deny his HIV status. He went through stages of excessive anger at former partners and at himself for the unprotected sex he had had since knowing how the virus was transmitted. He would alternate between this anger and lengthy periods of depression and withdrawal. He pulled away from his family and all of his friends, except Charlie, who one night succeeded in dragging Gordon to an HIV-positive support group. At the start of the meeting he sat sullen and detached, but by the end of the evening he was in tears, ready to face up to his infection with the support of others like himself. Eventually, he saw the need to assume responsibility for his wellness and began attending classes on proper diet and medication as well as initiating an exercise and meditation program in his daily life.

One day an invitation came to the support group from the local college for volunteers to speak on a panel of people who had been exposed to the AIDS virus. Up to this time, Gordon had remained exceedingly private about his status. He somehow knew, however, that acceptance of this invitation represented a threshold for further growth and self-esteem. By speaking publicly, he could give meaning to his own potential illness as well as becoming a resource for others in dealing with the virus.

He decided to accept the college's invitation, and, during this first of many speeches, he became aware that the virus no longer had the hold on him that it once did. In the process of assisting others, he was able not only to take control of his own life but also to give it meaning.

Gordon's experience once again demonstrates how a public step that is integrally related to the initial loss is essential to achieving a shift in the amount and kind of energy invested in the loss. Gordon's image of a long, healthy, and meaningful life was challenged by the AIDS virus. By accepting the invitation to educate others, he was able to recognize new meaning in the face of his precarious health status. Likewise, his "coming out of the closet" in regard to his positive HIV test represented an assumption of responsibility for his own health and welfare and for that of others.

Returning Home

Rhonda grew up in a small town in South Dakota, knowing she was different. Her high school years were miserable. She was whispered about behind her back, avoided in the locker room when suiting up for P.E., and excluded from every party and social function. She knew she was called a dyke and that her peers were snickering about her friendship with Lorene, a rather plain, homespun girl who lived on a farm some miles out of town. The truth of the matter was that their friendship was based on the fact that none of the other students wanted to have anything to do with either of them. To Rhonda's knowledge, Lorene was not lesbian like she, but there was no way to deflate the rumors that hounded her until she left town after graduation.

When the invitation to the twentieth high school reunion came in the mail, Rhonda knew that for her own good she had to go and finally make peace with the past. Over the past twenty years, she had struggled with the bitterness and resentment that were left from her high school days. With the help of therapy, maturity, and her lesbian friends, she came to realize that she had to return home and integrate the loss of her past.

On the night of the high school reunion, Rhonda tried hard to convince herself how important it was to walk into the old high school gym. She was nearly sick to her stomach and her knees were shaking, but she knew this was the opportunity to look into the eyes of her former tormenters and finally release their power over her self-esteem. She took a deep breath and entered her past. She slowly made her way around the room and, one by one, faced each person who had so painfully rejected her many years ago. As she approached each, she took his or her hand, greeted that person cordially, and said quietly to herself, "I forgive you." As she expected, a few were not even able to look into her eyes, but most were congenial in return. One woman, whom she remembered as having been particularly vicious, even surprised Rhonda by asking her for forgiveness. As Rhonda proceeded around the room, she could feel herself becoming lighter, as though the energy that had been consumed by her rejection and resentment was gradually being relinquished.

To say goodbye to the past, individuals sometimes choose to return to it physically as well as symbolically. When Rhonda received the invitation to reunite with her high school peers, she knew that she was being presented with an opportunity to put the losses and trauma associated with her high school years behind her. By returning home and looking into the eyes of those who had helped to destroy her life image of belonging, Rhonda was able finally to release the pain and bitterness of the past and move on. By taking a public step to integrate her loss, she enhanced her sense of self, making it possible for her to belong to other groups in more meaningful and healthy ways in the future.

Making Amends

Sonny married the first man he fell in love with. He and Raymond moved in together within a month of having met each other on their very first visit to a gay bar. Both were twenty-one years old and afraid of being identified as gay. They kept to themselves during their year together, assuming a "two-against-the-world" mentality. Then, with little forewarning, Raymond announced one day that he could no longer live like an outcast and that he was going to begin dating women and eventually settle down like a "respectable man."

Sonny's response to Raymond's abrupt departure from his life was to amass a quantity of pills and booze and barricade himself from outside contact. Three days later, after repeated telephone calls, Sonny's mother broke into his apartment and found him on the floor near death. He was hospitalized for a month, with his parents assuming all the costs because the insurance would not cover a suicide attempt. The accumulated bills exhausted their savings and forced them to take a second mortgage on their house.

With the help of counseling and a twelve-step program, eventually Sonny was able to get on with his life. He became comfortable enough with his own sexuality and had addressed the issues surrounding his suicide attempt enough to volunteer to work on a gay and lesbian hotline where many of the callers were young people contemplating taking their own lives.

When his parents grew older and their health failed, their financial resources had dwindled to such an extent that they were unable to afford nursing care in their own home and would need to enter a convalescent hospital. Sonny knew that his suicide attempt many years before had depleted their savings and had largely contributed to their present dilemma. Although he had verbally asked for and received their forgiveness a long time before this, he now felt he needed to make amends in a way more directly related to the sacrifice his parents had made for him. It was now his turn to take a second mortgage on his home; with the money from this, he hired a home health service to look after his ailing parents.

Sonny's public step was twofold. His volunteering with the gay and lesbian hotline represented his willingness to give back to the gay community by presenting himself as a sign of hopefulness following his own suicide attempt. His second avenue of integration was to stand by his parents in their time of need in much the same way they had stood by him. He had imagined himself as a faithful partner and dutiful son, but when both images collapsed, his loss was great. In assimilating those losses and bringing his cycle of grief to an end, he needed to make amends to life itself by serving those on the brink of suicide and to make restitution to his parents by taking care of them. By performing these actions, he was in a better position to experience his loss from a clearer vantage point.

Summary

People who have moved through their losses to the phase of loss integration experience a diminished concentration or intensity of pain and grief. Rather, they feel a tension or inner necessity to combine action with awareness. Seeing their losses with increasing clarity, they perceive a need to do something to symbolize the passage through and beyond the loss with a step of integration. Such an action in a sense ritualizes their transition to another phase in the process of transforming loss.

Life Image. Throughout the preceding chapters, all the individuals involved suffered the loss of their life images and blueprints for the future. The people in this chapter, however, are different from the others in that they are taking the first fragile steps necessary to restore a more viable and personally appropriate life dream.

Jill envisioned a long life with Abby, Harold saw himself as a respected and validated grandchild, and Jack and Mary wanted a married heterosexual daughter with children. Gordon quite naturally sought a long, healthy, and meaningful life, while Rhonda simply desired to belong and have happy memories of high school. Finally, Sonny's goal was to be a faithful partner and a dutiful son. They all struggled to gain perspective with regard to their shattered life images and they all accepted the invitation to integrate their losses in an active manner.

Reactions. The major characteristics of this phase are both the willingness to act and the actual taking of a discernible public step. By this movement, an individual can loosen the tension that was tied up in the loss and thus release the energy necessary to pursue a revitalized life image.

Jill felt that her lawsuit would restore her sense of justice and honor her commitment to her dead lover. Harold needed to forgive his grandfather regardless of his grandfather's acceptance of that forgiveness, while, for their

157

own integrity, Jack and Mary chose to be more honest in expressing their pride in their lesbian daughter. Gordon gave new meaning to his life by coming out of the shadows regarding his HIV status, and Rhonda endowed herself with a new lease on life by returning home and releasing bitterness. And Sonny's public steps took the form of serving others like himself and making amends to his parents.

Lessons. The integration of loss follows time spent balancing the various aspects of the loss and gaining perspective. After reflection, people often feel compelled to take some form of public step. The following lessons are offered to assist with this transition.

1. In many cases, grief can be rechanneled by an appropriate act of forgiveness of yourself and/or others.

2. If you have gained perspective on a loss, a public step or gesture becomes an almost compelling necessity; for your own integrity, you will ineluctably be drawn toward some act of justice making.

3. You take a public step not for some anticipated response from others, but for the deep gratification of knowing that somehow it will help you assimilate the loss.

4. There are often many possible and appropriate steps of integration rather than one perfect one.

5. Don't fret if many opportunities for public steps pass you by; but likewise don't hesitate too long, because changing circumstances may make integration of the loss increasingly more difficult.

6. Because losses are often so multifaceted, it may take many discernible public steps, perhaps over time, to address the many aspects of the loss.

7. An appropriate public step can constitute a viable counterbalance to years of closeted shame and secrecy.

9

Reformulating Loss

The process of reformulating loss can take place only after some type of integration has occurred. This reframing shifts energy away from the loss and allows for the emergence of a more authentic life image for gay men and lesbians. In this process, the original loss or losses that had set the phases in motion are viewed from a new, more positive perspective. What had once seemed so painful and devastating is now seen as having provided the gateway to freedom and rebirth.

The people in this chapter all exhibit a newfound feeling of vitality, an experience of having come alive again. Having unburdened themselves by means of a symbolic public step, the energy that was once consumed by their loss is now available to be redirected to other, more creative endeavors. Accompanying this is a sense of flowing with life, an almost childlike wonder, and a rootedness in the present. This new centeredness permits these six individuals to live more spontaneously and keeps them from being tied to the tyranny of scripted, future outcomes.

Working Through Shame

Chet was a married salesman who had worked the rest rooms at highway truck stops for years. Like many others, he was a gay man trapped in a heterosexual marriage, and anonymous sex with men seemed to him the only outlet for his sexual longings. Through the 1970s and into the 1980s, he had innumerable sex partners, and he probably would have continued this habit had it not been for the AIDS epidemic. Chet's self-image was very much tied to being a successful conqueror of other men. He enjoyed the excitement of the chase and was so proficient that he was rarely turned down. When he found himself so frightened of possible disease that he couldn't perform sexually, he felt he needed to get tested so he could see if he had been exposed to the virus.

Chet's negative test both relieved and depressed him. He thought to himself, "Why me? Why have I escaped? Guys with fewer tricks than I've had have been infected." Chet felt strongly that God must have spared him for some purpose. He immediately vowed to be a faithful husband to his wife, Phyllis, and to make up to her for his deceit and for all the nights she had spent alone. However, his good intentions lasted only a short time; he soon found himself feeling overwhelmed by his cravings to connect sexually with other men. The thought of never again doing this depressed him and led him to seek counseling.

Chet's counselor forced him to talk about many of the incidents that he had never shared with anyone. As he worked through his secrecy and shame, he could see the continual caring in her eyes and was thus better able to accept himself. During the many months of counseling, he came to recognize how he had dichotomized his sexuality, placing his gay orientation in the shadows and his pseudo-straight sexuality in the socially sanctioned institution of marriage. He knew that he had to bring his gay side out of the dark by talking to Phyllis about his true nature and his secret life. This step into the light helped him resolve his loss and allowed him to gain a new sense of meaning and self-respect.

Chet came to value himself as a gay man and reframed his sexual compulsions as a genuine need to relate sexually with other men. He knew he could no longer deny this essential part of himself and still retain his integrity. Phyllis was aware of his growing consciousness and was willing to stay with him and explore the possibility of renegotiating the nature and structure of their relationship. With Chet's shame and secret life no longer an issue, they were able to approach their relationship without illusions and with an openness to new perspectives.

Chet's HIV test was a mixed blessing, bringing him both relief and the realization that he needed to confront his life image as a conqueror of other men. When he lost his way of life in the shadows, he also lost his way of being with other men. Only by taking the step of seeking counseling and working through the shame of acting out in darkened rest rooms was he able to bring into the light the goodness inherent in his desire to connect with other men. With this reformulation, he was freed to be more open and authentic with Phyllis, future partners, and himself. Turning the darkness into light empowered him to reframe his life image from that of a conqueror, or user, to that of a person striving for genuine relationships with other human beings.

Being Freed From Jail

Stella took pride in the fact that she was one of the first women accepted as a police officer in her city. She had chosen this profession not only because she liked the work but also because it met her need for protective structures behind which to hide her lesbian identity. She organized her life to protect her secret and liked having a job in which her role and the rules of behavior were clearly defined.

Following several incidents of gay-bashing in the city, the gay and lesbian community organized a series of demonstrations in front of the station to protest what they perceived as police inaction against the perpetrators. Stella was on duty in the front office during one of the protests and overheard several of her fellow officers mocking the demonstrators with comments such as "You wouldn't catch me risking my life for a queer."

This incident and the reaction of her colleagues constituted for Stella a moment of truth. Something within her was released, and she instantly realized that she had suffered a profound loss. The illusion that she could insulate herself from her sexuality was shattered; she knew she could no longer maintain her pretense of heterosexuality. When her attempts to either hold on to or let go of her life image no longer seemed to be working and full awareness of her loss set in, she decided to see if the local lesbian support group could help her. In her characteristically structured manner, she promised herself that she would stay with the group for three months. By the end of that time, she knew that her integrity compelled her to stand with her gay brothers and lesbian sisters at the next police station demonstration.

A month later, when Stella took her place in the protest march outside the station, she felt free of the oppression of secrecy, fear, and duplicity that had long plagued her. Fellow officers hassled her the next day at work about participating with "those queers" and tarnishing the image of "the fine police force in our city." To this she replied: "We prefer to be known as lesbian, and I have the right as a citizen to assemble peacefully in my off-duty time." She added that if they continued their remarks, she would file official complaints that clearly documented their harassment of her with the union and government authorities.

As Stella could have predicted, the division within the police force was intense and split between admiring supporters and determined opponents. She commented to some of her friends that she was watching her worst fears become reality as articles about her appeared in the local papers, controversy surrounded her, and rumors and complaints concerning her lifestyle abounded. There were attempts at demotion, but the union stood by her, explaining that her performance at work did not warrant such action.

Throughout this ordeal, Stella often felt tired and beleaguered, but at the same time, she felt herself gaining a sense of purpose, strength, and freedom as she confronted what she had long avoided. She had met the dragon and it didn't slay her. As her humor returned, she was able to joke half-seriously that "what this city needs is a good lesbian sheriff." Ironically, Stella had never felt lighter in her life.

Both Chet and Stella challenged fear and found it to be the doorway to freedom. Fear had confined Stella to a self-imposed jail. Only when the illusions that composed her life image were destroyed was she able to reformulate her self-identity and her vision of the future. By taking the public step of joining the demonstrations in front of the police station, Stella entered her worst nightmare. Her carefully structured existence was replaced by a swirl of publicity, controversy, and harassment. Yet she not only survived it but also grew in the process. She came to realize that if she could live through this ordeal, she could deal with almost any adversity. Thus, she emerged with a renewed sense of strength and hope, as well as the foundations of a reframed, lesbian life image.

Seeing Life Through a New Lens

Marty's life had revolved almost exclusively around his mother since his senior year in high school. It was at that time that Mary, his widowed mother, began exhibiting symptoms of early-onset Alzheimer's disease. His attempts to take classes at the local community college proved futile because he could not leave Mary at home alone. She would wander off, burn herself on the stove, or leave the bath water running while she went outside in the nude. They had no money for care and their few friends were unable to provide the twenty-four-hour vigilance that Mary required. Marty had dreams of embarking on a career in photography, which had been encouraged by the many awards he had received for his work as a sports photographer for the high school yearbook and newspaper. His mother's illness forced him to abandon his hopes.

His older sister told him that she couldn't take care of Mary because she needed to be free to find a husband and start a family. Knowing about his orientation, she said to him: "Look, you're gay and won't be out looking for someone to marry. So I guess you're elected to take care of Mom." Thus, Marty sacrificed his dreams of a career in photography out of a sense of love and obligation toward his mother.

During the remaining ten years of Mary's life, Marty devoted his time to her care. He was barely able to read photography magazines and was afraid to hope too much for fear his dreams were lost forever. Perhaps to fill the emptiness caused by his grief, he ate continuously, until he was one hundred pounds overweight.

While Marty was recovering from his mother's death, he started attending classes at the community college again. Not surprisingly, though with a great deal of apprehension, he gravitated toward the photography courses, where his professor soon recognized his talent. One day, the teacher suggested that Marty apply to a professional photography school. He was accepted, and there he came alive and began realizing his potential as both an artist and a human being. After having been isolated for so many years, he felt a deep need for relationships and started socializing with his fellow students. He saw that his weight might be putting his health in jeopardy, so he joined Overeaters Anonymous.

As he developed friendships and lost weight, Marty began to feel a new lease on life. His photographic eye became keener, and his instructors encouraged him to exhibit his works in galleries. He particularly excelled at taking photographic portraits of his gay and lesbian friends, many of whom were quite successful in the photography industry. His skill at capturing the gay soul on film eventually led to his being commissioned by a publishing house to undertake an assignment of photographing gay men and lesbians around the world. Marty's professional and personal accomplishments made him feel that he had been reborn. Both his relationships and his photography gave witness to a sense of joy and playfulness. On film, he learned to capture the wonders of nature and the beauty of humanity.

Marty, like Chet and Stella, was eventually able to reformulate his life image. As is the case with so many gay men and lesbians, the care of his mother fell upon him, necessitating that he abandon his life dream for what might have been many more years. The inertia in the prime of his life could have left Marty socially isolated, chronically overweight, and bereft of a vocational life image. Had he not taken the public steps of returning to school, initiating friendships, and attending Overeaters Anonymous, Marty might not have been able to revitalize and reshape his life image to fit his gay spirit. His dreams of photographing sports events were reformulated to the reality of capturing people like himself on film. Through this more personally authentic way of engaging himself, he was able to see life through a new lens and bring his hopes to life again.

Reframing Assumptions

Mai's parents were Asian immigrants who scrimped and saved to pay her way to the best schools. For as long as she could remember, Mai had wanted to be a teacher, a mentor to the next generation. Her parents had drummed into her head the conviction that if you work hard and get a good education, you'll reach your goal. This was the assumption that guided her life and career preparation.

While Mai was in college, she came to terms with her lesbian nature and joined the Gay and Lesbian Union on campus. She was honored when her peers elected her secretary. After graduation, she applied for teaching jobs, and her applications invariably occasioned reference checks. Somehow the recruiters from the prospective school districts discovered her membership in the Gay and Lesbian Union, and not once was she offered an interview.

After much soul-searching, disillusionment, and bitterness, Mai began the process of reformulating her assumptions. She was confronted with the stark reality that in the teaching profession, hard work would rarely guarantee admission if you were openly lesbian. The assumption that had so long guided her ambitions proved to be illusory. The loss of this lodestar of her life caused her immense grief, but it also proved to be the starting point for new opportunities.

When Mai took the step of applying for entrance into a graduate program in counseling, she knew she was turning the corner on her loss. She felt a sense of freedom and integrity as she embarked upon a course of study that would allow her to mentor men and women like herself.

She knew she had a great deal to offer about the pitfalls of formulating life images based on assumptions that are less than viable for lesbians and gay men.

Many of the assumptions that form the basis for life images are deceptive when applied to people of same-gender orientation. Mai needed to reframe her belief that by working hard she could eventually attain her goal. After much pain, she was able to reformulate this assumption. She continued working hard, but this time for something that was attainable, rather than for something that might have been more possible for a person with a heterosexually based life image. The step of applying to the counseling program was integral to Mai's reframing of her assumptions and reformulation of her life image.

Exploring New Connections

Cole, a fifty-year-old gay man, had been searching for a suitable life partner for thirty years. His only successes proved to be brief relationships. Like many gay or lesbian people who deeply fear further rejection, he felt he needed to mold himself to please whomever he was courting. In explaining his frequent failures in love to friends, Cole would often elaborate in great detail on how hard he tried, how much he gave, and how little was reciprocated.

A potential lover did him a favor one day, even though at the time it felt to Cole like a stab in the heart. Elliott said to him, "Cole, you're a nice guy, almost too nice, but don't you have any opinions of your own? You're a chameleon." This hurt Cole deeply and caused him to go into a state of depression. However, after much internal dialogue, he eventually came to see that Elliott was absolutely correct and that one of Cole's assumptions about life was that to be loved he had to be pleasing. This belief left him with little personality of his own and a great deal of anxiety as to whether or not he was saying or doing the "right" thing. He knew that for his own happiness, and possibly for his survival, he had to do something.

At his earliest opportunity, Cole drove to the nearest urban center, located the best gay bookstore, and purchased several books that talked about friends, self-assertion, relationships, loving someone gay, living alone, and dealing with feelings. He read voraciously, heeded the pointers in the books, and tried to put them into practice. Additionally, Cole sought out workshops on assertive behavior and living gay/living single.

Gradually, Cole began to make new friends who appreciated him for who he was. He learned to be genuine and to express his feelings more clearly and appropriately. Most important, Cole learned to connect with himself and others in new and fresh ways. He never did find a lover, but it didn't seem to matter as much any more.

Cole's life image included having a long-term, mutually nurturing relationship. He sabotaged this dream on a regular basis by failing to present to potential lovers an authentic personality with whom they could relate. Like Mai, he was operating under the direction of a nonviable assumption; his was that being pleasing to another is a prerequisite to being loved. Elliott's comments delivered the death blow to Cole's illusions and set him on a passage through loss. His turning point was getting in the car and driving to the bookstore. This trip initiated a movement to connect with himself and others in a deeper and more emotionally authentic way. By following through with what he was learning in the literature, he diminished his anxiety about how he appeared to others. As a result, he was able to reframe his concept of love and to understand that to be loved, he first had to love himself. Most important, he was able to reformulate his expectations about connections and relationships.

Flowing With Life

Julie was an early leader in the lesbian movement in her mid-sized Texas city. She was continually trying to push her sisters out of the closet, where most of them lived for fear of losing their jobs. Having inherited her parents' cattle business after their deaths, she had no fear of being fired. In fact, she was well respected in the community as a savvy businesswoman who executed smart deals and kept her word. She made no bones about the fact that she was lesbian and was often heard to say to anyone who was around: "I like women as much as the next cowpoke."

Julie's four years at the university majoring in agribusiness and animal husbandry offered her the chance to be influenced by and be a part of the burgeoning lesbian movement in the 1970s. She returned home after graduation with a sense of urgency to spread the message of lesbian liberation. She formed a lesbian consciousness-raising group and immediately began educating the other members about the destructive effect their staying closeted had on the entire lesbian movement. The harder she pushed, the more they resisted her politics and heatedly insisted that she had no idea what it was like to live with the constant fear of being fired. She responded with anger and impatience at what she termed "their chicken-shit way of dealing with life."

The problem came to a head one night when the group unanimously told Julie that unless she backed off, she would no longer be welcome. The women made it clear to her that she was pushing them faster than they were willing to go and that they had serious problems with her rigid single-mindedness, intensity, and aggressiveness. She listened to these words in stunned silence and walked out, vowing never to return.

The next few weeks saw Julie raging at "those ungrateful chicken-shits." In her mind, she called them "stupid bitches," and she constantly faulted them for reading so little lesbian literature or failing to acquaint themselves with what was happening in the broader movement. She dismissed both them and their attitudes with the words: "Go ahead and live in your closets. I don't need to waste my time with you. Good riddance!"

Eventually, however, Julie grew tired of being just one of the cowboys, and she came to realize how deeply she missed her lesbian sisters. For the first time since the death of her parents, she cried and felt terribly alone.

After many months of grieving over her loss, Julie began to appreciate what the women had been trying to tell her. She saw that they were not rejecting her or the notion that the movement needed as many visible lesbian role models as possible; they were just not ready yet to be as open as she. They were understandably frightened, and

the time was not yet right for them. In a letter she carefully composed to them, Julie acknowledged their fears and
her pushiness and thanked them for slowing her down.
She told them that the incident made her stop and examine her anger and how it got in the way of her effective-
ness in speaking for the lesbian movement. Further, she
admitted that this anger was negatively affecting her
health and that their forthrightness had compelled her to
begin changing her life.

Julie rejoined the lesbian consciousness group, but
this time she began hearing her sisters' concerns from a
fresh perspective. The practice of daily meditation
allowed her to center herself and released her from the
need to control their lives and the focus of their discussions. She maintained many of her opinions and was still
frank in expressing them, but it seemed as though the
anger surrounding them had dissipated. Julie became
more comfortable letting events take their course without
the compulsion to invest energy scripting an outcome. As
she allowed the intensity within her to be lowered and
her expectations to be more open-ended, she was better
able to appreciate each person for who she was and each
moment as it unfolded. She found that what she had
failed to accomplish by aggressive persuasion, she was
now more effectively achieving with her patience, mutual-
ity, and willingness to nurture.

Julie saw herself as a leader of the lesbian community
and was convinced that she could change attitudes and
behaviors if she acted aggressively, confronted her sisters
on the errors of their ways, and spoke persuasively on
politically correct lesbian behavior. Thus, according to her

life image she was an evangelist for the lesbian cause. It was only when the enactment of this vision was soundly rejected by those she most needed to champion that Julie was able to begin the painful process of reformulating her raison d'être. The letter was an important public step toward a more integrated way of relating to her sisters. By allowing life to unfold rather than forcing or controlling it, Julie found flowing through herself a vision of a more mutually life-giving lesbian leadership.

Summary

Once the public step of integration has been taken, an experience of revitalization often occurs. At earlier stages of loss, people feel a sense of death and debilitation, but at this stage it is as if a resurrection and an empowerment has taken place. With this rebirth, individuals get on track again, but often at a level that is more connected to their feelings and that allows them to feel more at one with themselves. From this position of centeredness, they are able to appreciate the opportunities for growth that have resulted from their losses. For the first time in a long while, they feel energized and ready to live and dream once again.

Life Image. The cases in this chapter demonstrate that the reformulation of a life image often entails a shifting of that image to bring it into configuration with a deeper or more authentic self. Some may see this process as bringing themselves into harmony with the divine Wisdom.

Chet reformulated his assumptions about sexuality as his life image of himself shifted from conqueror of men to a person striving for a genuine relationship with the masculine. Stella's loss precipitated a change in the image she had of herself as a rule-bound, role-defined protector of public order to a protector of her own integrity and that of her lesbian sisters and gay brothers. Marty's task was not as much to reformulate a new life image as to resurrect and then add nuances to a dream that had once seemed dead. Mai viewed herself as a mentor to the next generation; by reformulating her notions of hard work and successful outcome, she was able to see herself as a counselor rather than as a teacher. Cole's image of himself in relationships was altered from that of a people pleaser to one of a man with more authentic connections with himself and thus with others. Julie reformulated her assumptions about leadership; hence, her image of herself as lesbian evangelist shifted to a less aggressive and more centered vision of leadership.

Reactions. A common thread running through the loss reformulation phase is the freedom felt by these individuals. Their commitment to authenticity resulted from having made a decision to confront head-on the obstacle that was blocking the fuller assimilation of their loss and, hence, their path toward growth. Chet's willingness to deal with his shadow sexuality led to a loosening of his dichotomization or his "gay = bad versus straight = good" way of looking at the world. Stella met her most-feared dragons of rejection, insecurity, and ridicule, and emerged with the prizes of strength and renewed purpose. Marty overcame inertia to bring his hopes alive again, and Mai challenged deep-rooted assumptions in order to mentor others in a manner more congruent with her sexual orientation and integrity. By doing everything he knew possible to modify his people-pleasing behavior, Cole succeeded in

176

connecting with himself and won his self-esteem in the process. Finally, Julie not only swallowed her pride by writing a letter and rejoining the group, but, more important, began through meditation to embrace her inner wisdom, quiet her anger, and find her center.

Lessons. Once a public step has been taken, it is easier to reframe loss and to see life from a new perspective. The following lessons are offered to assist in the redirection of energy to new endeavors and the restoration of purpose and meaning that are the hallmarks of this stage.

1. Eventually, you can come to see that no occurrence in life is entirely constructive or destructive, positive or negative; everything can be used for growth—even your losses.

2. Once you have experienced a loss worse than death and survived, you never need fear dying in the same way again.

3. If you allow honesty to illuminate your path through loss, you can make your way through the darkness of shame into the light of integrity.

4. Just as despair breeds stagnation in the earlier phases of loss, so also will inertia forestall the refashioning of your life image.

5. Sometimes a seemingly nonviable life image isn't entirely unworkable; it merely needs to be reviewed, reshaped, and revitalized.

6. Your negative assumptions about yourself can hinder healing; concentrate rather on loving yourself enough to move beyond fear.

7. Paying attention to your deepest self and listening to your inner wisdom leads to the authenticity necessary for reformulating and eventually transforming loss.

10

Transforming Loss

The pathway lesbian and gay people take in transforming loss can be viewed in much the same way as the process of developing faith described by James Fowler.[1] As individuals journey through loss, they experience an expansion of their vision that allows them to see more deeply, beyond the meaning of events and into the hearts of other people. Paralleling this is an increased intimacy with one's true self, with others, with the global community, and with the Spirit who weaves it all together. Up to this point in the phases of loss, the journey has been fairly solitary. With the reformulation of loss and its release of energy, there is a movement away from self-absorption and toward reinvolvement with the community and a deepening concern for the interconnectedness of all human beings.

A shift to a different plane, a mysterious metamorphosis, seems to occur between the stages of reformulating and transforming loss. When a person has reformulated loss, something deep within her or him comes together, disparate elements are consolidated, and there is an emotional sense of closure. Many people are able to identify a moment, a point of enlightenment, when suddenly their vision became crystal clear. What had once been vitally important to their image of life itself no longer seems to matter. The search for the meaning of the loss is no longer necessary. They feel released from what once bound them and open to whatever happens.

It is important to note at this point that no loss is completely transformed in such a way that the individual arrives at some perfect completion of a loss cycle. In this lifetime there is no idyllic state in which a person is finished grieving once and for all. Rather, loss and gain go hand in hand; each time the integration of loss brings a new perspective, an old perspective is lost and must be grieved for. As life images are constructed and then dismantled, the good news is that transformed loss occasions an increased openness and fluidity in the face of change and a greater willingness to surrender the ego to the Ultimate Wisdom.

This chapter introduces six individuals who have experienced devastating losses. As a result of the process of reformulating these losses, they are able to balance the dichotomous and disparate elements of life, see the interrelatedness of all things, and feel a deep sense of empathy and oneness with other human beings. No longer bound by the confines of an expected life image and having reformulated their original one into a more fluid form, their vision of community and justice is expanding. Likewise, being less emotionally attached to material strivings and objects, they are freer to appreciate the symbolic and the mystical. Finally, in transforming the loss, the individuals in their own ways are becoming integrated with the Energy Source and allowing its wisdom to empower and work through them.

Interrelating All Things

Randy Blue Cloud from very early in his life had had a sense that his destiny was different, even from that of other Native Americans. Missionaries had converted his family to Christianity, so when it was time to go to school, he was sent to the Christian boarding school rather than the Native American one usually attended by the kids from his New Mexico reservation. With his bookish manner and quiet ways, he was an outsider in most social groups. His classmates liked and respected him but rarely felt comfortable including him in their activities. He was happiest when he was in church surrounded by sacred things. He knew that when he grew up, God wanted him to be a holy man like the kindly minister of his church. In high school, he came to suspect that he was what the books described as a homosexual. He shared this worry with the minister, who told Randy that this was a way God was testing his faith and to remember that he had not been given a cross too heavy to bear.

After high school graduation, Randy Blue Cloud entered the seminary to pursue his dream of becoming a holy man. He expected this time to be the most joyous and fulfilling of his life, but instead he found himself gradually becoming depressed. Although he couldn't say why, he was unsettled and saddened by what he was learning in seminary classes. He was told of the evil that surrounds us, of a judging and distant God, of "man's" dominion over the earth, of the need to convert Native Americans and other nonbelievers, and of the gulf between earth and heaven, spirit and body. Further, he heard that homosexuals were sinful and that they needed

181

to repent and turn their lives over to Jesus if they were to be saved.

Something deep inside told him that none of this was true. He could hear the medicine man of his childhood saying that the Great Spirit was present in everything and that even mountains and stones were sacred. He reasoned from this that his sexuality must also be holy. He felt he was being torn between the ancient lore of his past and the teachings in his seminary courses. His depression became so pronounced that he decided to take a leave of absence and return home to his reservation. He felt he had to follow the voice deep within him.

In the process of his healing, Randy joined in the rituals of his tribe. He entered the holy ground and took part in sweat ceremonies, participated in the tribal dances, and sought out the wisdom of the elders. It was there that he met Walking Bear, a medicine man, who heard the agony of his soul. Randy felt sufficiently drawn to him that he confessed his sexual orientation, to which Walking Bear replied: "Many of us called by the Great Spirit are given this gift." He then told Randy the stories of the gay shamans and berdaches of the many Indian tribes and helped Randy appreciate and take pride in his sacred heritage.

Randy stayed near Walking Bear for the next year, listening to the stories of the earth and learning that holy people such as themselves are the hands and feet of the Great Spirit. Randy was struck by the interdependence of all things, animate and inanimate, and the graceful interplay between Father Sun and Mother Earth.

After a time, Randy knew he had to undertake a vision quest in order to discover his own path and what he was to bring back to his people. While on his quest at Red Mesa, the Coyote befriended him and became his connection with the animal Spirit. Coyote, the Spirit of contraries, reminded him that as a gay man, the source of his power was in his difference and in his representing the wily, whimsical side of the Great Spirit. Randy returned from his vision quest with the name "Eye in the Sky" because of his ability to see beyond and reconcile opposites. As was his tribal custom, he told only Walking Bear of his name and of the destiny he finally realized was his.

Randy Blue Cloud sent the seminary a letter of resignation, telling his former teachers that he felt called to set out on a path of bringing gay and lesbian Native Americans into oneness with their souls, with the earth, and with their tribal heritage. Through the years, he put into writing many of the stories Walking Bear had told him, including those of the berdaches and gay shamans. His ability to see with a different eye invested his talks on college campuses and before gay and lesbian Native American groups with a spirit of vision and an awe at the relatedness of all life forms. He became known as a holy man, though a far different kind from the one of his original image.

Randy's dream of being a Christian holy man like the minister of his youth seemed to vanish when he experienced the discrepancy between the seminary teaching and the echoes of the Great Spirit within him. His loss came when he became depressed and needed to let go of the seminary and return to the reservation to gain perspective. His meetings both with Walking Bear and later with

Coyote on the vision quest empowered him to take the public step of claiming his gay identity and resigning from the seminary. With newfound energy, Randy was able to allow the emergence of a more viable and reformulated life image of a holy man. This reframing transformed his vision and empowered him to be the "Eye in the Sky" for others, enabling them to see beyond their disconnectedness from self, others, and the Earth to the oneness of all things.

Moving From Meaninglessness to Mentoring

Throughout high school, Carol suspected her sexual orientation was toward women. This troubled her deeply, because more than anything else, she wanted to be "normal," to date boys, and eventually to have a family of her own. Her secret made her keep to herself, and when it came time to look for a job after graduation, she made certain it was one in which she could be virtually invisible so as to hide her sexuality.

Carol had been an inventory clerk in a windowless warehouse for five years when the growing company decided to hire another woman to help in the office. She was attracted to Patsy the first day she met her. It soon became apparent that the sentiment was mutual, but because they were both Christian, their belief systems and accompanying guilt prevented them from acting on their emotions. Carol felt trapped and tormented by her feelings. It seemed there was no place to go to get away from herself, and even the windowless warehouse was no longer safe. She needed to get rid of the poison inside of her, so she quit her job and sought help.

Carol recalled hearing Pastor Albin praising the work of a Christian counselor, Dr. Howell, with people who had problems such as hers. The next day she made an appointment and was relieved when Dr. Howell could see her immediately. He was very comforting and assured her of God's love for "all his children," no matter who they were or what they had done. He also told her that God had helped her catch this problem before she acted on it, which made it much more likely that she could be cured. He had her write down her dreams and then helped her attach heterosexual endings to them.

After many sessions with Dr. Howell, Carol decided it was time to begin dating men through her church. She was encouraged to believe that if she just found the right man, he would help her to be and feel "normal." She went out with several men, keeping in mind that, as a Christian, she needed to save herself for marriage. This never became an issue, however, since even the simple act of kissing them made her sick to her stomach. The more she tried to become heterosexual, the more hopeless she felt, until she thought that she was losing her mind.

One day, in desperation, Carol called Patsy, whom she had not seen since she had left the warehouse. Patsy told her that she too had felt that she was coming apart, but God helped her by sending her to a wonderful church in town where she could be both lesbian and Christian. On the next Sunday, Carol joined her friend at the service, where she was exhilarated at being surrounded by people like herself, singing the songs of her childhood, and hearing her orientation affirmed in prayer.

Through her involvement in the church, Carol began to grow both personally and spiritually. For the first time since she could remember, she felt she was part of a group and allowed herself to trust these people and be nurtured by them. In this atmosphere, she felt sufficiently supported to break out of her shell and become an active participant in life. She agreed to read Scriptures and play her guitar at services, took a job working at a foster home for delinquent girls, and began dating other women. With these activities, she could feel herself awakening inside, growing in self-confidence, and coming alive to the rich possibilities arising before her.

Carol began to experience an abiding sense of God's presence in her life and the unshakable belief that she was unconditionally loved by her Creator. At work, she could sometimes feel this love flowing from herself to the girls in the home. It soon became apparent to her that she had a gift for mentoring homeless young women, especially those who had left home or had been thrown out because of their sexual orientation. She knew that her life work was to open a home to serve girls who were as troubled and isolated as she once was.

Even though it took her years to accomplish her dream, Carol finally made it. Once the home was open and the first residents were safely settled, Carol felt a spiritual groundedness. Just as God had included her in love, so also was she including the young women she mentored. As she was loved to her very depths, divine love flowed through her to them. This deep sense of empathy gave meaning to her life and provided a redefinition of the concept of family for her.

Carol wanted from life what most people desire, a "normal" relationship that would lead to a "normal" family.

She thought that being lesbian deprived her of this, so she hated herself and felt isolated and depressed. In order to avoid painful reality and hold on to her life image, she went to therapy, prayed, and dated men. But these efforts proved futile. It was only when she was on the brink of a mental breakdown that she took the step of calling Patsy and attending a lesbian-affirming church that helped Carol reconcile her religion with her sexuality. This synthesis breathed new life into her. Thus energized, she emerged from her protective shell and began to trust herself and others. Most profoundly, she began to experience the Creator's love in her life and the call to reflect that love in her work with homeless young lesbians. In the process of this spiritual transformation, she had reformulated her life image of a family and was thus able to cooperate with God's love in moving from meaninglessness to mentoring.

Connecting Life With Death

Joe had been a successful clothes salesman before the effects of HIV infection rendered his employment problematic. Some days he felt fine, but on other days he couldn't even drag himself out of bed. When he first found out that he was exposed to the virus, he was terrified. But once he overcame his initial shock, he began to fight by keeping himself updated on medical advances and actively involving himself in a local HIV support group. His emotions, however, were all over the map. At one moment he would rationally engage his physician on the phone about his T-cell count, and shortly thereafter, he would be raging and seeking revenge on the person who might have exposed him to the virus.

In spite of his best efforts and the antiviral medications he faithfully took, tests indicated that his immune system was becoming weaker. After he first experienced a case of oral thrush, it dawned on him that maybe the beginning of the end was in sight and that his image of a long life was slipping away. He mourned this awareness with tears and intense pain. Something in him, nevertheless, knew that his grief was older than the loss he was currently experiencing. As he sat with his feeling, images of his deceased parents floated to consciousness, and instinctively he knew that he needed to connect with them.

As soon as he could make the arrangements, Joe flew to Kansas City, where his parents were buried side by side. Many years earlier he had left home, having never divulged his gay identity for fear of how much it would hurt them. He had been mustering his courage to tell them the truth when they were killed in an automobile accident. While at their grave site, he reflected on the fact that he had had no opportunity to share with them the stories of his life and what it meant to him to be gay. He felt a sense of regret, loneliness, and deep sorrow. Thus, he once again mourned their passing as well as the fragility of his own life.

While Joe was seated on the grass between his deceased parents, he had what he would later describe as a mystical experience. He could feel their living presence within him and surrounding him and was absolutely reassured that they were as alive as he was at that moment. Additionally, he knew that some loving Power was encompassing them and eternally intertwining their lives. At that moment, he knew they were all being embraced.

Something compelled Joe to return to the cemetery the next day. As he walked amidst the gravestones, he was aware of the same presence he had experienced the day before. He could feel what he described as the Spirit connecting him to his Irish immigrant grandparents; his first lover, Stan, who had been killed in Vietnam; Aunt Charlotte, who gave him his first puppy; Cousin Don, who helped him build the treehouse; his babysitter, Ruth, who taught him to read; the adults in the neighborhood where he grew up; and many of the people who formed the tapestry of his childhood memories. Joe sensed that their living energy was with him then and would continue to enliven and renew him in his remaining days of life and beyond.

The abiding presence of a loving God and special people and the absolute knowledge of life's continuity gave Joe a new lease on life. Because of his experience at the Kansas City cemetery, he was convinced that life existed on a continuum and that death was merely a transformation in attachments. He radiated this certainty, and others who had been exposed to the AIDS virus sought him out for the revitalization that his presence brought them. Joe's own connections with life remained tenuous, but each day he felt the Spirit weaving him and his loved ones together in a timeless web of past, present, and future, life and death.

Joe, quite naturally, had imagined a long life for himself. The AIDS virus challenged that assumption. He fought with the resources he had at hand, but eventually he came to the painful awareness that death was a possibility. At this point, he could have easily lost all hope and passively descended into despair. But some intuition called him to the gravesites of his parents and others from his childhood. Joe's public step allowed him to view death not as a severing of life but as a continuation into which someday he would be welcomed by a community of loved ones who had gone before him. This transformation enabled him to see life and death from a different plane, one where there are no boundaries and where all existence is connected by the hand of a loving Spirit. Joe felt more alive than ever before and sensed that the future held much promise and hope for him.

Being Reborn to Empathy

Lupe had to fight for her education and for her image as an independent woman with a career of her own. It made her very angry that in her culture a woman was expected to submit her needs to those of her family. Each fall she had to beg to go to school, since her parents worked in the fields and expected her to stay home and watch her younger brothers and sisters. As she was growing up, Lupe felt different from her peers, who always seemed to be talking about boyfriends and babies. This made her more determined than ever to have a life of her own someday and not exist as someone else's property.

Lupe was so driven by her dreams that whenever household duties weren't taking up her time, she was studying, often until the early hours of the morning. Her grades were so uniformly excellent that the high school counselor helped her to win a full college scholarship, complete with a work-study program for room and board.

Her parents insisted that she turn down this honor, but she refused and angrily left home.

Lupe was the only Latina at the eastern women's college that had granted her the scholarship. She was ashamed of her ethnic and socioeconomic roots and was determined to fit in with the rich and privileged white girls who were now her classmates. She chose to major in English literature because it put distance between her and her background of poverty. She even tried to lose what little traces of the Spanish accent she still had.

Lupe's anger at her own past and at what she considered patriarchal oppression led her to the feminist consciousness group on campus. It was there that she met other lesbians and began to understand her lifetime feelings of difference from the majority of women. She developed an awareness of herself as lesbian and came to appreciate the universal subjugation of women, but she did so from the vantage point of a privileged white Anglo-Saxon. It was from this perspective and eventually with a Ph.D. that she took her first university job as an assistant professor of English literature, worlds away from the fields of her childhood.

During her years of education and early employment, Lupe had only minimal contact with her family. One day she received a phone call from her mother telling her that her older brother, Carlos, had been killed in an agricultural accident. Lupe knew she had to return home for the funeral and finally confront her past.

Lupe was standing with her family at the rosary, and as she was looking down at Carlos in the open coffin, something snapped within her. The face that she saw before her was the same face that she had so often looked at many years ago while being sexually molested. The power of this long-buried realization stunned her and forced her to sit down to collect herself. Throughout the funeral and the subsequent family gatherings, she couldn't dispel the recurring memories of her brother and his abuse of her. They came in waves and at times overwhelmed her.

Lupe knew she had to get back to the university and meet with her counselor as soon as possible. Her illusion of superiority within her culture had collapsed, and she could no longer distance herself from the reality of her origins. Rather than continuing to flee her past, she had to come to terms with her own victimization and early loss of self. Lupe painfully worked through her grief in therapy and eventually came to feel the angry shell that had protected her in the past melting away. In its place came a softening. She eventually found within herself the ability to forgive her brother, who she realized was also a victim, both of poverty and of the cult of machismo in their culture.

As Lupe became more in touch with herself, she could feel her empathy toward others deepening and expanding. Through her own personal hardship, she came to a deep identification with other victimized people of her culture. With this new appreciation of her Hispanic heritage, she found herself desiring to hear the stories of other women like herself. By listening, she came to realize that the mainstream of society oppressed and marginalized Hispanics, lesbians, and non-Hispanic heterosexual women in very similar ways. And Hispanic lesbians found themselves in a situation of "triple jeopardy." This insight led her to start a small theater group for Latina lesbians, where women could read their poetry, perform their plays, and tell their stories.

Lupe's professional focus underwent a transformation. Her teaching and writing interest shifted from the field of English literature to that of Latin American literature. Out of her own woundedness, she was enabled to empathize with the agony of other oppressed people of Hispanic cultures. The unblocking of her personal pain occasioned a releasing of her own creativity. Her sterile journal articles were replaced by stories and poetry of rebirth, liberation, and resurrection.

Lupe had a life image of herself as an independent woman who was superior to and different and separate from her family and others in her culture. She imagined that she could achieve her potential by simply severing ties and moving forward into a promising future without ever having to look back to a painful past. She wanted no part of a heritage that she characterized as one of poverty and ignorance, especially as it dealt with women. It was only when she saw Carlos in his coffin that she began to realize that she was as victimized as the others in her culture. In fact, with the passage of time, Lupe became aware that she suffered a triple marginalization as a woman, a Latina, and a lesbian. Her loss was a loss of an illusion of superiority and separateness from her culture. The public step of starting a theater group signaled a growing identification and bonding with her people, as well as an appreciation of the richness of her heritage. By embracing this richness, she was able to reframe her image of herself as an independent woman and to see that her strength came out of her heritage and not apart from it. At the death of the driven, denying, angry academic came her resurrection as a compassionate, openhearted, and inclusive companion of the oppressed. Her pain was transformed into a deep understanding of the human condition that allowed Lupe to feel a profound sense of empathy.

Surrendering Self to God

Grant's domain was Bodybuilders Gym, where he worked as an attendant. Even when he wasn't on duty, he spent almost all of his free time there, lifting weights, working out, and enjoying the other beautiful male bodies. His life goal was to achieve the image of perfect masculinity. He could not understand, being as physically attractive as he was, why he failed to find a lover. After all, lots of the guys thought he was "hot" and wanted to take him home for the night. Occasionally, he would accommodate them. One evening at a local bar, two guys asked if they could join him for some three-way sex at Grant's apartment. This appealed to Grant because they had great bodies, but they turned out to be real animals. Not only were they high on crack cocaine, but they put Grant into restraints, beat him senseless, robbed his apartment, and left him for dead. When Grant didn't show up at work the next day and failed to call, his boss came looking for him. He would have died had help not arrived when it did.

Grant had lost a great deal of blood and had suffered major damage to his spinal cord. After spending six weeks in ICU, his condition was sufficiently stabilized for him to be sent to a rehabilitation center. His physicians had told him that he would never walk again, but he was determined to prove them wrong. After all, life without a well-conditioned body was not worth living. He threw himself into his rehab exercises with the same zeal and determination he had once devoted to bodybuilding. But one day, after continually failing to achieve the goals he had set for himself, he realized that the doctors were right. He would not walk again. This awareness sent him into deep despair, and he tried in numerous ways to kill himself, but the vigilance of the hospital attendants always prevented his death.

Grant then became withdrawn, sometimes sitting and staring out the window for hours. His image of the perfect body was in shambles and his worst fear had become a reality. He now had to confront the shallowness and emptiness that resided inside his once beautifully sculpted physique. He was terrified, vulnerable, and helpless, not knowing what would become of him. At last he wept uncontrollably.

Rabbi Cohen was the resident chaplain on duty one day when Grant was sitting in his wheelchair on the patio. The rabbi pulled up a chair and asked him if he would like to talk. Grant nodded and began to tell the chaplain about what had happened to him.

Rabbi Cohen listened intently, and when his turn came to respond, he told Grant his story. Just as Grant had wanted to be the perfect and best bodybuilder, he too had once wanted to be the perfect and holiest rabbi. After alcoholism had taken its toll on his life and he had lost nearly everything, including his rabbinical dreams and ambitions, he had grieved much as Grant was now grieving. Rabbi Cohen then related how devastated he had felt at losing his role and the expectations he had about himself. He had known that he was at the brink and that there was nothing left to do but call upon God and let God lead him through his fear and loss.

Grant heard what the chaplain said and knew that he too had to surrender his self-image and face his fears. He asked the rabbi to help him deal with his terror by teaching him a prayer. Grant always remembered the words of Psalm 86 that Rabbi Cohen wrote down for him that day:

Bow down thine ear, O LORD, hear me: for I am poor and needy.

In the day of my trouble I will call upon thee: for thou wilt answer me.

Teach me thy way, O LORD; I will walk in thy truth. (Ps. 86: 1, 7, 11)

Grant said these words daily during his recovery, sometimes even hourly during the painful physical therapy sessions in which he learned to adjust to life in a wheelchair.

After Grant left the hospital and returned home, he eventually was able to capitalize on his skills of fixing things with his still-strong hands by starting a small appliance repair shop in his garage. Over time, his sense of self-esteem and confidence increased, and he began to relate to his physical being in a very different way as shifts occurred within him. He saw that his body was God's temple and that what dwelt within was even more beautiful than anything he had outwardly manifested in his bodybuilding days. He learned to see beyond the body and derived strength from the disabled children he

196

helped coach for the Special Olympics. By squarely facing his own fear of physical imperfection, he was able to transcend his disability and to accept whatever God had in store for him.

Grant aspired to an image of perfect, physical masculinity. He devoted nearly his entire life to attaining this goal by spending hours at the gym, pumping iron. This image was destroyed as a result of his assault and subsequent lifetime confinement to a wheelchair. Fear and despair nearly overcame him when all his laborious attempts to walk proved futile. His bargaining ended when the full awareness of his loss set in, and internal recovery began with the public step of asking Rabbi Cohen for perspective and prayer.

By reframing his life image of outward physical perfection, Grant was able to shift his focus inward and to relate to his body and psyche in a more authentic and harmonious way. This reformulation allowed him to experience God's power within him where once there had been only emptiness. His spinal cord injury required him to face his greatest fears of physical imperfection and disability and rise above them. It was by transcending his physical being that he was able to surrender himself to God and thus achieve a form of perfection he could never have imagined.

Healing Into Wholeness

Patricia had won the Religion Award at St. Boniface High School. All her teachers knew how earnestly she desired to be a nun and acknowledged that she had the character and disposition of a wonderful religious sister. Patricia attended daily mass, was the first to volunteer for work with the poor and needy, and was consistently the pleasant and perfect lady.

No one was surprised when Patricia did enter the convent upon graduation from high school. She was happy there and seemed to glow whenever her family and friends came for Sunday visitation. The most joyful day of her life was when she made her solemn profession of vows and was given the name Sister Mary Patricia.

Since entering the convent, however, she had been noticing within herself feelings of warmth and attraction when working alongside some of her sisters. These emotions bothered her because she didn't understand them, and they were the only troublesome aspect of her otherwise serene existence. One of her constant companions was Sister Cecelia, with whom she served on the same hospital shift, kitchen rotation, and softball team. Sister Mary Patricia yearned to spend as much time as possible with Sister Cecelia and thought of her constantly when they were apart. She imagined them taking walks together, holding hands, and giving each other back rubs. It horrified her to realize that she was in love for the very first time—and with a woman!

Sister Mary Patricia vowed to stay away from the temptation of Sister Cecelia and offered to join her pain to that of the suffering Christ on the cross. One day while she was reciting her devotions in the garden, Sister Cecelia approached her and asked why she was so cold and distant of late. Sister Cecelia told her how much she missed talking with her and eventually confessed that she had fallen in love with her and that the distance between them was tearing her apart. They ended up in tears in each other's arms, feeling both exhilarated and terrified. They made love later that evening but woke up the next morning feeling ashamed, guilty, and sinful for having violated their vows of chastity. Sister Cecelia requested and received an immediate transfer to a hospital position that had opened up on the opposite coast. With Sister Cecelia gone, Sister Mary Patricia was miserable. She tried fasting, prayer, and spiritual guidance in order to restore her enthusiasm for the image of sisterhood she had so long espoused. But nothing looked good, not even life itself.

Patricia left the convent deep in despair, with her dreams and hopes dead. She felt so empty inside that she contemplated taking her own life. With the only vocation she had ever loved no longer a choice for her and with the option of a lesbian relationship not a possibility within her church, she felt doubly bereft. She saw no hope for life-giving work or love in her future and could not tolerate the thought of living another day. Had she not had strong religious convictions, she would have attempted suicide.

Patricia tried to live her life as a celibate lesbian, as the church expected. She clung to the belief that all that she needed for her happiness was a relationship with God that was more intimate than any she could have with a human being. She continued her practice of daily mass and prayer and forced herself to join the Catholic singles group. There she met a nice man in whom she tried to develop an interest, to no avail. In fact, nothing seemed to be working, neither celibacy nor dating men. She looked back at this period as being the bleakest in her life, and she remembered asking herself repeatedly how a loving

God could condemn a lesbian to a partnerless life, devoid of intimate love. She felt that the God she knew would not demand such an unreasonable sacrifice.

Patricia had already read the Catholic writers who supported the Church's stand on mandatory celibacy for lesbians and gays, so she now turned to those theologians and spiritual writers of her faith who provided scripturally based but more gay-affirming interpretations. She sought out as many books as she could find in the city's gay and lesbian bookstore and ordered others from catalogs she found there. Gradually, she came to believe that a lesbian relationship was morally conscionable and theologically correct within her faith tradition. Furthermore, she saw that God was inviting her to dare to believe that such a relationship was the Holy Spirit's will for her happiness. At this point she realized that her search for wholeness required that she place her trust in God and take the steps necessary to bring into harmony her spirituality and sexuality.

Patricia sought out the local chapter of Dignity, the organization for Catholic gay men and lesbians, and attended their mass the next Sunday. Being new to the group and somewhat nervous, she sat in the back and watched. What she saw felt deeply right to her. The sights and sounds of the religious tradition she loved so much were interwoven with images of lesbian and gay lovers and their friends openly embracing one another and standing around the altar of God. So many things came together for her that day that she resolved to try to bring the remainder of her life into the same spirit of harmony.

Christie entered Patricia's life several months later at another Dignity gathering. They were both dating other people at the time, so it took a while for them to get together. When they did, Patricia's relationship with Christie so energized her that she undertook the additional training in hospital administration she had long postponed. The profound healing Patricia was beginning to feel as a result of her bonding with Christie prompted her to want to heal other unresolved chapters of her life. She knew that the order of nuns to which she had belonged needed someone to run the infirmary for their sick and elderly sisters. The mother superior and governing board were overjoyed when she applied. Her subsequent work with them brought the closure she needed. In her original life image she had been affiliated with these holy women and had been serving others. She began to see that, while the nature of her affiliation, holiness, and service was different from what she had originally envisioned, her newfound life was more inclusive of her deepest nature.

Patricia and Christie had been feeling the need for a ceremony to ritualize and express their oneness. They planned a backyard ceremony for a morning in early September. Friends of theirs had decorated the yard with an array of plants and fall flowers, a member of the symphony played a violin in the background, and all the guests were gathered around a magnificent arch under which stood the special couple. Patricia had a sense of oneness as so much of her life merged that day. A special gay priest friend from Dignity pronounced God's blessing upon them and listened as they recited the vows they had written for each other. Patricia looked around and saw several of the sisters from the infirmary, her former lover Sister Cecelia, her lifetime physician and his wife, members of Dignity, two teachers from the hospital administration program at the university, several childhood chums, her parents, her siblings and their children, and her eighty-year-old grandmother. Her joy that day in some ways reminded her of what she had felt as she solemnly professed her vows to the sisterhood several years earlier. But it seemed deeper this time, more mature and inclusive of the totality of her being. It was as if she had healed and united the fragments of her life.

Patricia wished to dedicate herself to God and to the service of others by joining a religious order of women. This image began to crumble as she realized that she was lesbian and that she was in love with Sister Cecelia. The disparity between the life of a nun and the reality of her emotions led to such pain that she needed to leave the convent and let her dream die. She still attempted to hold on to the image of being a holy woman within the Catholic church by practicing celibacy and attending daily mass. The awareness that this was not working caused her such intense misery that she was forced to acknowledge the possibility that God was calling her to reframe her life as a lesbian woman. Her first trembling step was into a bookstore to discover an alternative way to live as a lesbian within her faith. This quest eventually guided her to Dignity, where she experienced a homecoming and an integration. Patricia's healing included not only balancing her spirituality and sexuality but also creating a new life image that reformulated her ideals of service to God and others alongside a community of holy women. The commitment ceremony served to symbolize joyfully the transformation of her loss as it gathered the disparate elements of Patricia's life into a moment of wholeness.

Summary

The newfound perspectives of challenge and creativity that come when loss is reformulated bring with them a shift to yet another vantage point where insight and vision are expanded. Energy that was initially unblocked with the public step of integrating loss now flows more freely and spirals people in this stage away from preoccupation with themselves and toward oneness with others and with the mind of God. From this plane they can see that nothing ever ends, that there is continuity and interconnectedness in all things, and that loss only alters the nature of relationships rather than severing ties completely. Individuals in this phase feel released from the constraints and expectations of a life image because they are present in the moment and open to the fluidity of experience. Life seems to flow, and dichotomies that once pulled them apart now seem more reconciled. Events, people, and even new losses are viewed as much more than concrete reality, as symbolic representations of a transformed level of meaning.

Life Image. Once people reformulate their life images, they experience a subtle but profound shift in the way they interpret information and view reality. For example, when Randy Blue Cloud was able to expand the boundaries of the sacred imposed by Christianity and its definition of a holy man, he was able to see beyond other contrary elements of life and into the harmony of their interrelatedness. Carol had to broaden her notion of what constitutes a family before she could appreciate that the mentoring of homeless children was the way her Creator's love was to move through her. Joe's reinterpretation of a long life produced within him a shift that allowed him to envision life and death on a continuum and his own passage through life as merely a process of altering attachments. As Lupe came to see that her independent life image needed to embrace the richness of her cultural heritage, she was opened to empathy not only for her own people but for all others who suffered. Once Grant was able to see the true perfection of his now-broken body, he felt empowered to rise above it and continue to surrender himself to the Source and Creator of that perfection. Patricia needed to reformulate her dream of being a servant of God and others within a community of women in order to bring the fragmented elements of her life into a state of wholeness.

Reactions. It is helpful to examine the variety of behaviors exhibited by the six individuals in this chapter in order to better understand how this phase of transformation translates into daily life. Connection or attachment both to God and to others appears to be a crucial element at this stage. All the individuals in some way gave back to others and served to affect the lives of others. Being transformed as a result of the loss of his or her life image and having been released from the striving to meet its assumptions, each was brought to a higher purpose. Randy Blue Cloud was called to be a storyteller and writer for gay and lesbian Native Americans. Carol's new family became the homeless lesbians she felt privileged to mentor. Joe's life-giving presence flowed out to others who were infected with HIV and gave them spiritual strength. Lupe left the persona of the detached academic and joined her pain with that of her Latina sisters in a theater group. By transcending his own physical being, Grant was able to see perfection in himself and in the disabled children he coached. And Patricia achieved wholeness as she worked as an openly partnered lesbian with her ill and elderly former sisters.

Lessons. When loss has been reformulated, a shift to a different plane of vision occurs. The following lessons emerge from the experiences of the people introduced in this chapter and may serve as guideposts in realizing the symbolic aspects of your loss.

1. Your original life image contains the seeds of transformation, but the protective coverings must first fall away in order for new life to flourish.

2. Spiritual transformation involves a surrender of yourself and an openness to the Ultimate Wisdom.

3. The realization that your worst tragedy has become the source of your greatest gain can help you better flow with life—no matter what happens.

4. You may find as you transform loss that the notion of loss itself is an illusion; in fact, what you grieved for is never essentially gone.

5. Once you have experienced loss and come to life again, you realize that nothing truly passes and that only the nature of your attachment changes.

6. Once you see a side of yourself in every other human, you can begin to appreciate the concepts of empathy and unconditional love.

7. In striving to live out a life image, you are restricted by a limited vision; with the shift of transformation you can see that all life is purposeful and interconnected.

Coming Out Within:

Reflections on Transformed Lesbian and Gay Spirituality

Interwoven throughout the process from initial awareness to transformation are a number of spiritual themes. This chapter will expand upon these as well as highlight some of the tasks involved in transforming a shattered life image.

Life As a Journey

All the events in a person's life are connected. What may seem to be randomly occurring elements actually are meaningfully interrelated. According to Patricia Weenolsen, "all the events of our lives, great and small, are inexorably driven" toward some ultimate purpose and our limited wisdom, or the wisdom of a higher power, "will see these seemingly disconnected happenings in some coherent pattern." The events of people's lives are not "merely random scraps of cloth gathered together in random piles, or tapestries whose theme we are too close to discern but whose every figure, thread, and stitch is essential to a unique, inevitable, and meaningful design."[1]

Wisdom can come to all, gay men and lesbians included. All our joys and losses, every moment of our lives can be rendered purposeful on Wisdom's broader level—even what at some past moment had appeared to be so wrenching, so perplexing, so foolish, so shameful, or so inconsistent.

Lesbians and gay men are drawn to see life from the vantage point of a higher Wisdom. From this perspective, they can see that efforts to assimilate with heterosexually focused life images have been a preparation for assuming their own unique life journeys. The losses, then, are an indispensable part of the path leading gay men and lesbians toward transformation. The death of so many friends to AIDS, the humiliation caused by public exposure of their orientation, rejection by society, and innumerable inner tensions all constitute the stepping-stones upon which they are invited to walk toward individuation.

Individuation is that process through which we journey to the core of our beings, of our selves. Within lesbians and gay men, as within all people, there is an instinct toward wholeness. But attempting to conform to the heterosexual world and remaining attached to its approval divides energy and diverts attention away from acting upon that instinct. The gay and lesbian soul yearns for oneness with the Divine and feels a desire to allow the God of Creation to embrace the God mirrored within. This uniting of the inner and outer experiences of the same God leads toward a wholeness. The self is complete when the lesbian or gay being images her or his core as holy and merged with the Divine.

The Path of the Journey

Recent evidence has shown that gay men and lesbians are not only capable of this individuation process but in some cases have shown a higher level of moral and spiritual development than heterosexuals.[2] Adversity, shame, and living with continual incongruity can either demoralize and psychologically destroy or provide the pathway for spiritual and moral development. Living on the margins, as so many lesbians and gay men do, can be sufficiently dissonant to provide the momentum for change in some of the following ways.

From Rigidity Toward Openness. Transformed spirituality is characterized by a constant leaning toward openness and away from rigidity. This quest often leads to the awareness that the spiritual messages inherent in collective human wisdom are as close to us as our daily experiences. Thus, the losses and disequilibrium of living as gay and lesbian, rather than being defeating, can evoke a vitality and an emerging sense of purpose. Clinging too rigidly to scripted outcomes or expectations of how heterosexually focused life images were to have evolved can limit the courage and spontaneity needed to move along a particular life course. By choosing to accept themselves as they are and risk moving away from the prevalent culture, gay men and lesbians can open themselves to life on its own terms and come to trust in the guidance of an inner wisdom.

From External Authority Toward Personal Integrity. Spiritually evolving people have begun balancing the notion of authority with that of personal responsibility and have initiated a movement from exterior regulation to interior transformation. As we come to rely on our own intuition, we become more capable of identifying and being guided by felt needs, values, and the dictates of a personal conscience. We have learned the lessons of balancing our needs with those of others, harmonizing personal integrity with legitimate authority, and blending assertiveness with the art of compromise and negotiation. In the lives of spiritually developing gay and lesbian individuals, the locus of authority has become more internal; hence, they are guided less by fear and conventionality and more by a sense of personal integrity.

From Disconnectedness Toward Interrelatedness. Lesbians and gay men who are in the process of transformation, in learning to accept objectively the events and losses of life, begin to appreciate how their losses have elements in common with those of all humans. Accompanying acceptance of life as a process comes the realization of the interconnectedness of all beings; thus, what happens to a gay man or to a lesbian happens to all members of the species in different ways and at different times. The awareness of the interrelatedness of their own history with the multiform life dramas of human experience brings gay and lesbian individuals to the point of identifying with the broader human species. Evolving lesbian and gay people know at some level that they are not excluded or disqualified from the human adventure due to sexual orientation and that the universal stories and myths of transformation are as applicable to them as they are to everyone else.

From Self-Centeredness Toward Generativity. Compassion and generativity are qualities of spiritually developing lesbian and gay people. A growing openness to the

stories of all men and women endows them with a vulnerability to the truths and claims of those who likewise live
on the margins of society. This widening of vision and
valuing brings about an expanding of the heart, a compassion. The pain and sense of loss that evolving lesbian and
gay individuals experience lead to a sensitivity to the suffering of others and a desire to share their gifts and blessings in support of anguished brothers and sisters. The
compassion for those who exhibit different traditions and
spiritualities and an awareness of the societal resistance
that can often accompany such differences result in a
broader world view. Rather than viewing oppression in
terms of culturally isolated phenomena, gay and lesbian
people who are transforming spiritually are seeing the fabric of global oppression that is woven not only through
their communities but also throughout the lives of all
those who live on the margins.

From Literal Toward Symbolic. Spiritually maturing
women and men reframe their losses in terms of a symbolic rather than a literal meaning. By having rendered
symbolic the events related to their suffering, developing
people of same-gender orientation are no longer prone to
concretizing or personalizing these events. Rather, they
perceive losses as prophetic, informing them of a larger
life's journey leading to unity and integration with the
One. They come to view events of pain and suffering as
messengers to the self about the self's path toward mystical communion with the Creator.

With the Abiding God

People working toward transformation usually have some
concept of a God, which may include God as divine

211

providence, the ultimate source of good in the universe, the one who sets life and energy in motion, the ground and stabilizing force of being, the life-giving Mother and sustainer of all things, or the holy Wisdom whose guidance weaves all seemingly disparate elements into oneness. Regardless of how God is understood or defined, the goodness and providence of a supreme being is reflected in the gay and lesbian soul. God has knit gay men and lesbians out of the fiber of her or his being and, as such, their sexual orientation reflects the image and likeness of the living God. God has created lesbian and gay people, and to do violence to them heaps contempt on their Creator.

God is love, and any relationship that reflects love reflects the source of love. Therefore, the loving relationships and unions of lesbians and gay men mirror the very essence of love, whose name is God. Just as God is present in love and joy, so is God present in all human pain and suffering. God is a colover and a cosufferer who accompanies humans on their individual journeys. Thus, Jesus Christ can be seen as the image of the suffering God, who, like gay men and lesbians, is continually crucified and offered the opportunity to transform anguish into new possibilities for life.

The notion of an unmovable God, existing in lofty splendor outside of *his* creation, being worshiped and feared from afar by pleading childlike creatures, is no longer a viable image for people growing and maturing through their losses. As we evolve, so also does our image and experience of God. Throughout this evolution and regardless of the eyes through which God is perceived, there is a deep "with-ness"[3] about God—a God who stays continually with all people, male and female, heterosexual and gay or lesbian.

The shaping stories and themes from Judeo-Christian scripture and tradition can and do apply to lesbian and gay individuals if viewed from the vantage point of mythology or metaphor. If looked at literally, these stories of faith appear to be applicable only to heterosexual journeys toward the Divine. Metaphorically, however, the virgin birth may symbolize the opening up of the spiritual possibilities in the gay or lesbian heart where once there may have existed only sterile fear, bitterness, and closeted shame. The imagery and metaphors found in the Song of Songs can be applied to the moral, sexual relationship of two gay men or two lesbians who love each other and can in fact reflect a mystical experience of the Divine.[4] The ascension of Jesus into heaven can come to symbolize a journey not simply into outer space but into inward space, to the place from which lesbian and gay people find their source, the dynamic consciousness within.[5] Thus, gay and lesbian individuals can claim the stories of faith as their own and find embedded within the motifs of religious tradition life maps and images that facilitate oneness with the abiding God.

Through Duality to Integrity

Unitive rather than dualistic imagery is conducive to spiritual integrity and transformation. For too long, lesbian and gay people have been depicted in negatively dichotomous terms as evil rather than good, sinful rather than holy, contaminated rather than clean, abnormal rather than normal, and unacceptable rather than acceptable. Hearing these terms with sufficient frequency, lesbians and gay men come to believe them, internalize them, and act according to their dictates. They can become convinced that they are indeed evil and contaminated, that their sexual lifestyle is debased, that their spirit has been condemned by God, that eternity is not possible, and that all that is left is the transitory pleasure of the moment.

In order to preserve the integrity of their being and see reality more clearly, transformed gay men and lesbians must learn to view themselves and their orientation in terms of both/and rather than either/or thinking. Every human being is a blending of right and wrong, good and evil, male and female, acceptable and unacceptable, gay and straight. Such a unitive blending can help them appreciate both their spirituality and their sexuality and how the two complement each other. Likewise, such an integrative consciousness enables gay men to embrace their feminine and lesbians to celebrate their masculine. By moving away from concrete, either/or, one-dimensional conceptualizations and moving toward both/and thinking, lesbian and gay people can open up their consciousness to the broad spectrum of possibilities inherent within all situations.

A particularly destructive form of dualistic thinking at work in the lives of many gay and lesbian individuals is the belief that the past can be depicted in largely negative terms and, hence, be forever scorned and disavowed. In reality, every past contains elements of good and bad, sanctity and sinfulness, and no past can be repressed, forgotten, or left totally behind. Since the past is interwoven into the very fabric of the present, the shame, the painful memories and humiliation, and the inner tapes of parents and clergy at their very worst can be integrated with the good and achieve the same benefits for learning and growth as those parts that are overtly treasured. All individuals are made up of both wheat and chaff, and any effort to separate these elements and disavow an undesirable part can prove damaging to wholeness, integrity, and spiritual transformation.

The Passage From Death to Life

For centuries, gay men and lesbians have lived with death, both psychic and physical. In earlier cultures, they were accorded the role of "midwives" or companions for those who were dying to a new birth. In later Judeo-Christian civilization, they were cast to the margins of society to suffer the slow internal death of being the rejected, the biblical *anawim* or exiled. Today, people of same-gender orientation are still very much the outsiders of the culture, and their alienation once again puts them in a unique position to choose for themselves a qualitatively different life image. In other words, having little to lose in terms of status, respectability, or prestige, they can begin to see themselves as having been released from society's strictures. Losses can become gains, and deaths can become resurrections.

Joseph Campbell has said that nature can be a teacher for humanity about life and death, because much of the life sequence in nature is identical to that of the human life.[6] Nature can also serve as a metaphor for the psychic life of humans. Motifs of death and rebirth thread themselves through the natural order—snakes lose their skins as they change and grow, caterpillars seem to die in their

215

burial shrouds in order to emerge as butterflies, and branches and leaves wither and die to give room for new ones to take their place.

This cycle of death and rebirth has profound relevance for gay men and lesbians. Their many emotional deaths and their living in the midst of death may prove a fitting preparation for personal transformation and the rebirth of a viable life image. The losses endured by lesbian and gay people can be seen as avenues to birth and becoming; the loss of normalcy, respectability, community, family, and friends, as well as the losses experienced in the physical deaths from AIDS, suicide, and addictions, can be vehicles to transcendence. The very proximity of gays and lesbians to crucifixion and death endows them with a proximity to resurrection.

The deathlike losses suffered by lesbian and gay people can be reframed as passages from one era or life state into another. These transitions, much like birth, involve pain. While there may be a temptation to abort the journey and despair, we can take heart in that the lessons we need for transforming a shattered life image are present in the midst of our anguish. These seasons or passages may seem dislocating and endless, but each comes at its proper time and has its proper length, containing "strengths sufficient for either life's blows or blessings."[7]

Encountering the Dragon of Fear

Fear stands guard over the illusion and the denial that allow gay and lesbian people to hold on to their sense of belonging, respectability, and livelihood and to the tattered remnants of their life images in order to cope and function in a homophobic society. It is only when reality and illusion clash with sufficient impact that the weight of the dissonance and discordance becomes too heavy to bear, and denial, illusions, and life images are shattered. The disequilibrium inherent in this "bottoming out" propels gays and lesbians into the unknown and away from a former illusory life image.

In order to transform spiritually, gay men and lesbians have no choice but to undertake this passage. As long as they force themselves to fit into the narrow confines of a heterosexually oriented life image, they will continue to experience an inner feeling of disharmony and dissonance. The journey, then, is away from reliance on non-gay-affirming mores, belief systems, and signposts of acceptability and toward trusting an intuitive gay and lesbian wisdom.

Inevitably, fear is a companion through this passage, because the passage is *through* fear. At every juncture of the journey, lesbians and gay men encounter the dragon of fear threatening further rejection, abandonment, ridicule, isolation, loneliness, and even the possibility of eternal damnation. Fear can also prevent people from seeing the complementarity of positive and negative currents, or from seeing death/rebirth and loss/transformation as different but inseparable sides of Wisdom's coin.

As death and rebirth go hand in hand, so also do fear and trust. Just as the losses of gay men and lesbians can be the springboard for personal and spiritual transformation, so also can fear introduce them to trust. Gradually, by confronting individual dragons and learning that the dragon cannot truly destroy, they can come to believe that the world that seemed to have so bitterly betrayed them is indeed worthy of trust. Instead of viewing life as a curse, they begin to see life as a blessing, trusting that it is a journey toward a transformed self and life image, that an inner Wisdom is gracefully at work, and that God, who is continually present, accompanies them in the guise of this Wisdom.

Appendix

Observations on Using the Loss Model

In addition to reflecting on transformed lesbian and gay spirituality, we have other postmodel observations to share. It seems to us that, rather than leaving readers in the higher planes of transformation, it is wiser to end the book with a grounding in the practical and answer the question, "What do I do with all this?" Thus, we will finish by turning again to the loss model itself and addressing three areas that we believe may cause readers difficulty in application. The discussion and special cautions that follow will be in the areas of timing, feelings, and support and will be directed to both lesbians and gay men and to their families and friends.

Timing

It is important to remind readers again that people move through loss in a spiraling manner rather than in a linear, sequential way. This means that elements of an earlier stage can be found in a later one and vice versa. Likewise, aspects of several stages can occur simultaneously as people sometimes find themselves going back to aspects of an earlier stage before moving on. Rarely do individuals progress through grief in a stairstep manner, cleanly finishing one stage before moving to the next. Those who expect such a clear-cut process of discrete steps often become terribly upset because they are not grieving "correctly."

In the same vein, it is also true that people may be dealing with several losses or even different parts of the same loss at any given time. For the sake of illustration, we presented case studies in which individuals dealt with a singular loss, but in reality, people usually must cope with many losses simultaneously. You may recall our discussion in chapter 2 about the ripple effects of loss and the fact that losses come in waves, with each loss triggering several others. Some of these are readily identifiable, such as the loss of a job or a partner, while others are more symbolic, such as the loss of an illusion or a life image. For example, as Solomon is feeling intense sadness over his lover's death six months ago, he is bargaining about his lifestyle as a result of a diminished money flow; additionally, he is raging and trying to let go of a friend who he felt rejected him at his time of grief and is numbed by the response of the local church that refused to bury his lover; at the same time, he is feeling more settled about the death of his father that occurred three years ago. Most people, if they were in a situation like Solomon's, would feel that they were losing their minds. But such confusion and fragmentation are not unusual for gay men and lesbians as they confront the spiraling phenomenon of multiple and simultaneous losses.

Additionally, loss is never over completely. In fact, for every loss you endure, residuals will periodically return in the form of stray thoughts or unguarded emotions or even some sharp pangs that take you by surprise. These visitations can be quite disconcerting, especially when you feel you have "gotten over" that particular loss.

If this seems discouraging, remember that it is so only if you try to understand everything or to stay in control of the uncontrollable. It need not be disheartening, however, if you remember that the mind can let in only so much information at once and that the journey of moving through loss takes time. Nature has its own rhythm, and forcing or rushing may appear to terminate loss more quickly, when in fact the process has been arrested at the holding-on, letting-go, or gaining-perspective stages.

The issue of timing as it relates to moving through the loss model presents some important advice for lesbians and gay men. We have also included some special suggestions for family and friends who are supporting them through their seasons of grief.

For Lesbians and Gay Men

- Confusion is normal during the loss process, and sometimes you may feel as if you are losing your mind when confronted with myriad losses.

- It's okay not to comprehend at any particular point in the loss process all the thoughts, feelings, and behaviors that occur. Statements such as "I don't understand what is happening to me!" are quite common.

- There is no correct way to grieve. In fact, even a book such as this can be taken too literally and be used as a basis of comparison with your own imperfect way of grieving. Our book is meant to point out

221

where loss can take you, but how and when you get there is unique to you.

- Like a river, loss seems to have its own natural flow, and forcing yourself to swim against the current will either exhaust or drown you.

- Knowing the language of spiritual transformation does not necessarily mean that it has become a part of you. Holding the vision and imagery of transformation can often provide hope when you're in despair, but remember to stay in the moment so that true change can occur naturally.

- Wisdom has her own timing. Be patient with her, surrender to her wiser ways, and let her guide you.

For Family and Friends

- Stay calm when loved ones look as if they were coming apart during their loss process. If they appear to be in serious trouble, seek professional consultation; otherwise, be open and keep in mind that your presence can help them sort through their confusion.

- Avoid the tendency to try to "fix" your loved ones or solve their problems; your evaluation of when and how they need to recover may be very different from theirs.

- Be careful not to compare loved ones to yourself or to imply that they are not grieving quickly or correctly enough when you relate to them stories of your own losses.

- If it becomes apparent to you and to numerous others that a loved one has been stuck in a stage for an extensive period of time, you might consider professional help in order to discuss your perceptions and options.

- Avoid conspiring with your loved ones when they are limiting their awareness of loss by inappropriately denying, holding on, or letting go. They need to go through these stages, but indiscriminately agreeing with them on every point rather than simply listening can sometimes retard their loss process.

Feelings

Dealing with the feelings involved when multiple losses strike can be particularly difficult for lesbians and gay men. A lifetime of maintaining a heterosexual life image has often left them numb to their emotions and distrusting of their own intuition and other perceptive abilities. In order to stay safe in an often homophobic and rejecting world, gay and lesbian people have had to learn how to wear a mask and remain invisible. Jokes, news stories, religious condemnation, high school ridicule, and personal taunts could have been overwhelming had they not been in the habit of stifling their feelings of anger, sadness, hurt, and terror. A hostile environment combined with a lifetime pattern of protective denial frequently sets up for gay men and lesbians an emotional condition much like that found in a combat or trauma survivor.

Thus, when loss sufficient to shatter their life image occurs, lesbian and gay individuals often have a reduced ability to understand, locate, label, or communicate their emotions. Because each stage of recovery from loss

requires the addressing of certain feelings and the skills to
do so, gay men and lesbians are often doubly challenged.
For them, recovery from loss is also a recovery of the
ability to feel, to trust, to intuit, and to dream. Concurrent
with the transformation of loss comes a reimaging of their
very being and a freedom to present themselves unmasked
and congruent to the world.

We offer the following suggestions to gay men and
lesbians to aid in the recovery of their "selves" and their
feelings. We also give some pointers for family and
friends, who play a vital role in helping them through this
process.

For Lesbians and Gay Men

- Remember, it is not dangerous to feel feelings. In
  order to move toward recovery, you have to let
  emotions emerge unfiltered and uncensored.

- Instead of ignoring feelings when they do come, it's
  important to pay attention to them. Locate one emotion at a time, ascribe a one-word label to each, and
  say it out loud.

- During the loss process, you may be confronted with
  some of the most intense emotions you have so far
  allowed yourself to feel. Keep in mind that they are
  not enemies sent for your destruction but rather
  helpmates to assist you through your loss.

- Don't be overly concerned if you have a delayed
  emotional reaction to a situation or if emotions aren't
  present from time to time, because years of keeping
  them in check may have formed a habit that is difficult to break.

- You can help access and release your feelings by developing the abilities to laugh at yourself, to touch, to imagine, to enjoy music, and to appreciate and perhaps even become involved in the expressive arts.

- To recover, you will need to trust others and communicate your feelings with them; but beware of the temptation to find someone to take your pain away.

For Family and Friends

- Realize that gay and lesbian loved ones may be more inclined to express their emotions if you give them permission to do so. Don't be disappointed, though, if they either ignore your offer or find it difficult to articulate their feelings.

- Be prepared for anger, rejection, and maybe even accusation, especially during the letting-go stage of loss. Don't take it personally. Keep studying the loss model so that you know what to expect during the various phases and are not tempted to respond in kind.

- Some of the emotions that your lesbian or gay friends or family members may vent during the earlier stages of loss may not be polite, polished, or even civil; in fact, many may be downright rude, offensive, or possibly even frightening. Resist the impulse to censor, edit, or judge the appropriateness of their feelings.

- There is a fine line between allowing a grieving person to vent emotions and knowing how much you're willing to accept. If you've had enough, you can always leave the room.

- Having gay or lesbian loved ones may have affected your own life image. Try to keep the pain of your loss separate from theirs. Resist statements like "How could you do this to me?" Often the closer you are to people in a loss process, the greater will be their temptation to unload on you. Don't be surprised if years of pent-up injustice land in your lap. It's better to let it flow off you than either to absorb and remember it or to throw it back.

- There is a delicate balance between keeping communication with loved ones open without forcing yourself upon them and respecting the distance they wish to maintain without departing altogether.

Support

Support throughout the loss process is crucial for everyone but has a unique relevance for lesbians and gay men. As we discussed in the section on feelings, gay and lesbian people have frequently and habitually denied their feelings and have created a world inside themselves where no one else enters. Because of this emotional isolation, they have often been unable to enjoy the bene fits of social support that members of other minority groups often have. For example, a gay adolescent male who is called a fag rarely goes home and tells his parents of his pain, as might a black youth who is called a nigger. As a matter of fact, many lesbian and gay individuals don't know whom they can trust with their secret and thus turn to no one for wise counsel or advice. This emotional aloneness deprives them not only of the objective perspective that others can provide but also of guidance in navigating through life's perils.

Warm, accepting, and nonjudgmental companions are essential for the passage through loss and the eventual healing of a shattered life image. For gay men and lesbians, there may also exist the additional journey from a lonely inner world into a trusting, loving community where true support is available. Developing the trust, courage, and skills to venture into a possibly rejecting world is the first task toward finding eventual support. There comes a point when the suffocation caused by living in exile becomes unbearable, and this agony can give lesbian and gay people the momentum to risk opening their lives to something different. It is important to capitalize on this energy for change and to begin looking around for someone who can become an initial building block in a support structure. To get the courage to approach others, gay and lesbian individuals may need to remind themselves repeatedly that self-disclosure and mutual sharing are essential for recovery through loss.

People of same-gender orientation often will single out some family member or friend who, while not having been privy to their deepest inner thoughts and fears, has demonstrated kindness, interest, or wisdom. This special person may prove to be the vital link between isolation and a support system. It is in this initial contact that gay men and lesbians may gain the ability to trust and develop the rudimentary relationship skills necessary to explore other friendships more confidently.

Such disclosures by lesbian and gay loved ones may cause those in whom they confide some pain and loss of their own. They may experience confusion or disorientation and require support for themselves. Discovering that a lifetime friend or a child is gay can challenge and upset people, leading them to question virtually everything else about what they perceived to be true. Someone who believed that homosexuals were sick and sinful can feel considerable internal dissonance when confronted by a cherished and healthy companion or family member's lesbianism. We give some suggestions below regarding support in moving through losses such as these. We offer similar advice to gay men and lesbians.

For Lesbians and Gay Men

- In order to build trust, you must go slowly and network one person and one disclosure at a time. Watch the tendency to cling too tightly to one person lest you limit your ability to develop a wider support community.

- You may need to visit a nearby city in order to gain access to gay and lesbian resources. These may include support groups, religious organizations, and bookstores where you can find periodicals, newspapers, and mailing lists.

- In addition to needing support for yourself, your own journey toward healing requires that you listen to and assist others. Developing the ability to reach out and empathize is an essential ingredient for transformation.

- In the aftermath of losing one mask, it's not uncommon to try on several others for a while. Keep in mind that you are vulnerable and in need of affirmation and may be tempted to wear someone else's mask in order to have an identity.

- Allow yourself to trust your own instincts. In seeking the support of others, watch out for those who feel unhealthy for you, who undermine your self-esteem, or who treat you or your loss too glibly or callously.

For Family and Friends

- Treat respectfully and carefully the initial self-disclosures of your gay or lesbian loved ones. Remember that you may be one of the first with whom they have shared their hearts, and your support may prove vital to their willingness to trust others.

- If appropriate, be willing to disclose a loss of your own with the bereaved. Your sharing can honor their worth and self-esteem by demonstrating a trust in them; it also can provide a sense of hope as well as letting loved ones know that they are not alone in their struggle.

- Being present to gay and lesbian loved ones in their loss may stir up a number of strong reactions in you. Seek support for sorting out feelings in case you are being targeted for anger, used, dumped upon, invited in and then rejected, or drained dry.

- Find people in circumstances similar to your own to avoid feeling so alone. Organizations such as Parents and Friends of Lesbians and Gays (P-FLAG)[1] can help you understand your own pain, work through confusion, and transform your own loss.

Notes

Introduction

1. John Schneider, *Stress, Loss, and Grief* (Baltimore: University Park Press, 1984), 59–77, 103–249.

Chapter One: The Life Image

1. John Boswell, *Christianity, Social Tolerance, and Homosexuality* (Chicago: University of Chicago Press, 1980), 3–39.
2. Cited in Michael W. Ross, *The Married Homosexual Man* (London: Routledge & Kegan Paul, 1983), 1.
3. Boswell, *Christianity*, 3–39.
4. John Money, *Gay, Straight, and In-Between* (New York: Oxford University Press, 1988), 49–50.
5. Craig W. O'Neill and Kathleen Y. Ritter, "Who Leaves and Rejoins the Church?," *Human Development* 8 (Spring 1987): 34–36.
6. Kathleen Y. Ritter and Craig W. O'Neill, "Moving Through Loss: The Spiritual Journey of Gay Men and Lesbian Women," *Journal of Counseling and Development* 68 (September/October 1989): 10.
7. Cited in L. W. Rutledge, *Unnatural Quotations* (Boston: Alyson, 1988), 108.
8. Joseph Campbell, *The Power of Myth* (New York: Doubleday, 1988), 5, 31, 53.
9. Campbell, *Power of Myth*, 5.

231

Chapter Two: The Path to Transformation

1. Patricia Weenolsen, *Transcendence of Loss Over the Life Span* (New York: Hemisphere, 1988), 499.
2. Schneider, *Stress, Loss, and Grief,* 59–77, 103–249.

Chapter Five: Letting Go

1. Dana G. Finnegan and Emily B. McNally, *Dual Identities: Counseling Chemically Dependent Gay Men and Lesbians* (Center City, MN: Hazelden, 1987), 31; Thomas O. Ziebold and John E. Mongeon, eds., *Gay and Sober: Directions for Counseling and Therapy* (New York: Harrington Park Press, 1985), 5, 9–25.
2. Eric E. Rofes, *Lesbians, Gay Men and Suicide* (San Francisco: Grey Fox Press, 1983), 20.

Chapter Eight: Integrating Loss

1. Schneider, in *Stress, Loss, and Grief,* called this phase "resolving the loss." In a February 1991 conversation, he said that he now prefers the term *integrating loss,* since terms like *resolving* or *resolution* imply a closure or ending to a loss rather than an ongoing shifting of energy.
2. Parents and Friends of Lesbians and Gays
   P.O. Box 27605
   Washington, DC 20038

Chapter Ten: Transforming Loss

1. James W. Fowler, *Stages of Faith: The Psychology of Human Development and the Quest for Meaning* (San Francisco: Harper & Row, 1981), 119–213.

Chapter Eleven: Coming Out Within

1. Weenolsen, *Transcendence of Loss,* 222.
2. Lou A. Bordisso, "The Relationship Between Level of Moral Development and Sexual Orientation of Roman Catholic Priests," *Dissertation Abstracts International* 50 (1988): 3137 B; Henry R. Mitchell, "Moral Development and Sexual Orientation," *Dissertation Abstracts International* 44 (1983): 441 2A; Claire V. Wilson, "The Relationships of Sexual Orientation and Gender to Adult Moral Development," *Dissertation Abstracts International* 45 (1984):700–701 2B.
3. Matthew Fox, *Original Blessing* (Sante Fe, NM: Bear, 1983), 92.
4. John J. McNeill, *Taking a Chance on God* (Boston: Beacon Press, 1988), 155–56.
5. Campbell, *Power of Myth,* 56–57.
6. Campbell, *Power of Myth,* 102.
7. Fowler, *Stages of Faith,* 274.

Appendix

1. See P-FLAG address, chapter 8, note 2.

Additional Readings

Fortunato, John E. *Embracing the Exile: Healing Journeys of Gay Christians*. San Francisco: Harper & Row, 1982.

Glaser, Chris. *Come Home! Reclaiming Spirituality and Community as Gay Men and Lesbians*. San Francisco: Harper & Row, 1990.

————. *Uncommon Calling: A Gay Man's Struggle To Serve the Church*. San Francisco: Harper & Row, 1988.

Griffin, Carolyn Welch, Marian Wirth, and Arthur G. Wirth. *Beyond Acceptance: Parents of Lesbians and Gays Talk About Their Experiences*. Englewood Cliffs, NJ: Prentice-Hall, 1986.

Heyward, Carter. *Touching Our Strength: The Erotic as Power and the Love of God*. San Francisco: Harper & Row, 1989.

Kominars, Sheppard B. *Accepting Ourselves: The Twelve-Step Journey of Recovery from Addiction for Gay Men and Lesbians*. San Francisco: Harper & Row, 1989.

McNaught, Brian. *On Being Gay: Thoughts on Family, Faith, and Love*. New York: St. Martin's Press, 1988.

McNeill, John J. *The Church and the Homosexual*. 3d ed. Boston: Beacon Press, 1985.

Nugent, Robert, ed. *A Challenge to Love: Gay and Lesbian Catholics in the Church*. New York: Crossroad, 1983.

Perry, Troy. *The Lord is My Shepherd and He Knows I'm Gay*. Austin, TX: Liberty Press, 1972.

Uhrig, Larry J. *Sex Positive*. Boston: Alyson, 1986.

ADDITIONALREADINGS

Woods, Richard. *Another Kind of Love: Homosexuality and Spirituality.* 3d ed. Ft. Wayne, IN: Knoll, 1988.
Zanotti, Barbara, ed. *A Faith of One's Own: Explorations by Catholic Lesbians.* Trumansburg, New York: Crossing Press, 1986.